D0691010

FOR SUCH A
Time
AS THIS

FOR SUCH A

Time

AS THIS

Secrets of Strategic Living
from the Book of Esther

RAY C. STEDMAN

DISCOVERY HOUSE
PUBLISHERS®

Feeding the Soul with the Word of God

For Such a Time as This
© 2010 by Elaine Stedman
All rights reserved.

Discovery House Publishers is affiliated with RBC Ministries,
Grand Rapids, Michigan.

Discovery House books are distributed to the trade exclusively by
Barbour Publishing, Inc., Uhrichsville, Ohio.

Requests for permission to quote from this book should be directed to:
Permissions Department, Discovery House Publishers,
P.O. Box 3566, Grand Rapids, MI 49501 or contact us by e-mail
at permissionsdept@dhp.org.

Unless otherwise indicated, Scripture is from the HOLY BIBLE,
NEW INTERNATIONAL VERSION®, NIV®. Copyright © 1973,
1978, 1984 by Biblica, Inc.™ Used by permission of Zondervan.
All rights reserved worldwide. www.zondervan.com

Scripture marked NASB is from the NEW AMERICAN STANDARD
BIBLE®, Copyright © 1960, 1962, 1963, 1968, 1971, 1972, 1973,
1975, 1977, 1995 by The Lockman Foundation. Used by permission.

Scripture marked KJV is from The Holy Bible, King James Version.

Interior design by Sherri L. Hoffman

Library of Congress Cataloging-in-Publication Data

Stedman, Ray C.
    For such a time as this : secrets of strategic living from the book of
Esther / Ray C. Stedman.
        p. cm.
    Includes bibliographical references and index.
    ISBN 978-1-57293-378-1 (alk. paper)
    1. Bible. O.T. Esther—Commentaries. I. Title.
BS1375.53.S74 2010
222'.907--dc22   2010000344

Printed in the United States of America

11 12 13 14 15 / 10 9 8 7 6 5 4 3 2

CONTENTS

PUBLISHER'S PREFACE

From 1950 to 1990, Ray Stedman (1917–1992) served as pastor of Peninsula Bible Church in Palo Alto, California, where he was known and loved as a man of outstanding Bible knowledge, Christian integrity, warmth, and humility. Born in Temvik, North Dakota, Ray grew up on the rugged landscape of Montana. When he was a small child, his mother became ill and his father, a railroad man, abandoned the family. Ray grew up on his aunt's Montana farm from the time he was six. He came to know the Lord at age ten.

As a young man he lived in Chicago, Denver, Hawaii, and elsewhere. He enlisted in the Navy during World War II and often led Bible studies for civilians and Navy personnel. He sometimes preached on the radio in Hawaii. At the close of the war, Ray was married in Honolulu (he and his wife Elaine had first met in Great Falls, Montana). They returned to the mainland in 1946, and Ray graduated from Dallas Theological Seminary in 1950. After two summers of youth ministry with Dr. J. Vernon McGee, Ray traveled for several months with Dr. H. A. Ironside, pastor of The Moody Church in Chicago.

In 1950, Ray was called by the two-year-old Peninsula Bible Fellowship to serve as its first pastor. Peninsula Bible Fellowship became Peninsula Bible Church, and Ray served a forty-year tenure, retiring on April 30, 1990. During those years, Stedman authored a number of life-changing Christian books, including the classic work on the meaning and mission of the church, *Body Life*. He went into the presence of his Lord on October 7, 1992.

There is no other book in Scripture like the book of Esther, and Ray Stedman has left us an insightful perspective on this book that you will find nowhere else. He gives us a unique three-dimensional view of the book of Esther, examining the story from these three perspectives:

1. As a historical document of actual events that took place in the life of the Jewish people and the history of the Persian Empire

2. As a thrilling narrative of romance and suspense that reads like a gripping novel

3. As a parable of profound and practical spiritual truths for our everyday Christian lives

The book of Esther has amazing relevance for us in the turbulent, troubled times in which we live. This ancient-yet-timeless book speaks to us across the centuries and instructs us about how God wants us to live today, in the twenty-first century. Queen Esther faced challenges and threats that were every bit as apocalyptic as the perils we deal with each day. She confronted those challenges with the faith and courage that come from God alone. We have much to learn from her life—and the lessons of her life are embodied in these fascinating, encouraging pages.

If you are perplexed and troubled by the events of the world in which you live, this is the book for you. All the power, courage, and strength you need to live strategically and effectively for God are available to you— and the book of Esther will show you where to find them. Read these adventure-filled pages and discover God's plan to use you in a mighty way . . .

For such a time as this.

—Discovery House Publishers

1

I AM ONLY ONE

The Background

*W*hen I was growing up in Montana, people left their doors unlocked and their windows open at night, sleeping serenely and safely in their beds. Today we live behind doors that are locked and dead-bolted, with iron bars on our windows. The world has changed in many ways since I was a boy—and not for the better.

We live in a world plagued by war, terrorism, mass starvation, crime, pornography, child abuse, and every other form of human evil. Oh, there have been improvements in technology, in mechanical conveniences, in treatments of diseases and injuries. But in all of the aspects of our lives that really make us *human*—the way we treat each other, our respect for God and morality, our regard for human life—our society has become increasingly corrosive, demeaning, and destructive.

If an unborn child becomes inconvenient, we abort that child. If an aging parent becomes too much of a burden due to Alzheimer's or physical infirmity or some other medical condition, there are doctors and judges who will help us euthanize that parent.

Computer technology, which has the potential of doing so much good in the world, is increasingly used to destroy human lives and relationships through the propagation of pornography, including child pornography. Films and TV shows saturate our society with images of incredible violence, appalling immorality, and the destructive values of a godless culture.

Against such an onslaught of wickedness and inhumanity, we might feel overwhelmed, wondering, "What can one person do?" But God has never accepted that excuse from His people. The Scriptures give us many stories of great events that were shaped by the obedience of individual believers acting in response to God's call. Again and again in times of crisis and decision, God called a single individual to take a courageous stand and make a difference.

God called one individual, Joseph, to speak His words and carry out His will in the pagan land of Egypt. God called one individual, Moses, to confront Pharaoh and deliver the nation of Israel from bondage. God called one individual, Daniel, to take a lonely, courageous stand against the blasphemy of the prideful king in Babylon. God called one individual, Nehemiah, to lead His people back to their homeland to rebuild the walls of Jerusalem.

And here, in the book of Esther, we will see God call one Jewish woman during a time of great crisis and peril. We'll see Him use a selfless, obedient young woman to deliver a nation from genocide.

Many times in human history, God has searched for that one person who would be *His* person for a time of moral or spiritual crisis—and that person could not be found! The prophet Ezekiel records the Lord's lament, "I looked for a man among them who would build up the wall and stand before me in the gap on behalf of the land so I would not have to destroy it, *but I found none*" (Ezekiel 22:30, emphasis added). And the prophet Isaiah declared:

> The LORD looked and was displeased
> that there was no justice.
> He saw that there was *no one*,
> he was appalled that there was *no one* to intervene.
>   (Isaiah 59:15–16, emphasis added.)

What tragic words! God seeks a few bold followers who will stand in the gap, who will seek justice, who will speak His truth in our own time of crisis. What a tragedy it would be if He called *your* name—and you did not answer. What a tragedy it would be if you simply shrugged and said, "I'd like to help—but what can one person do?"

What can one person do? In his poem "Lend a Hand," Edward Everett Hale (1822–1909) offers a resounding answer to that question:

I am only one,
But still I am one.
I cannot do everything,
But still I can do something;
And because I cannot do everything
I will not refuse to do the something that I can do.

God seeks a few bold individuals who will say, "I am only one, but still I am one, and I will be God's instrument for such a time as this." Make sure that when God calls your name you are ready and willing to stand up and be counted.

AGAINST THE TRIUMPH OF EVIL

The story of Esther is the story of one faithful servant who answered God's call. This is not merely a quaint tale from a distant time and a remote culture. The story of Esther is profoundly relevant to our times and to our lives. The story of Esther is as much about *you* as it is about Esther. If you can read the story of Esther without being personally and profoundly changed, then you have completely missed the point of the story!

The key statement of the entire book of Esther—the one statement that expresses the theme of the story—is found in Esther 4:14, where Esther's cousin Mordecai says to her, "And who knows but that you have come to royal position for such a time as this?"

For such a time as this! God placed Esther in a strategic position for a purpose. And she was God's chosen instrument "for such a time as this."

And you, my friend, are also God's chosen instrument for such a time as this—for the time of crisis and peril in which you live. God may not have placed you in a *royal* position, as he did Esther. But he has placed you in a *strategic* position in your home, your neighborhood, your office or factory, your church, and your community. And God has placed you where you are for such a time as this.

Just as Esther could not afford to be passive but needed to yield herself to God's will, you and I must be willing to act in obedience to His will and His Word. As the Irish statesman Edmund Burke once wrote, "All that is necessary for the triumph of evil is for good men to do nothing."

LIKE A NOVEL

Esther is one of the most neglected books in the Bible. Many people have told me, "I don't think I've ever heard a sermon on the book of Esther." The book is neglected not only in the pulpit but also in most Christians' personal devotions and Scripture study.

This is amazing, because the book of Esther reads like a great novel. It has everything a good page-turning story should have—unforgettable characters, romance, intrigue, suspense, arch-villainy, murder, betrayal, action, and a thrilling climax. The book of Esther also has something that's hard to find in most novels today: A powerful theme, guaranteed to challenge and change you if you simply dwell in its truths and apply them to your life.

Oh, and one more thing: The book of Esther is unlike any other novel you have ever read in one important respect: This book is absolutely, literally *true*. This is a richly detailed account of actual historical events, and there are parallels between this account and other historical records of the time (such as the account of King Xerxes' invasion of Greece in *The Histories* of Herodotus).

The story of Queen Esther takes place in Persia, which corresponds to modern-day Iran, during a time when the people of Israel were held captive in that land. To this day, there is a sizable Jewish population living in the Muslim state of Iran—the Mizrahi (or "Eastern") Jews, who are descended from the Jews in Persia during the time of Esther.

The book of Esther tells us how the Jewish festival of Purim came to be—the celebration of the Jews' deliverance from the genocidal plot of Haman nearly 2,500 years ago. Also in this book we see the first major outbreak of the irrational, genocidal, anti-Semitic hatred that has so afflicted the Jewish people for centuries—right up to our own time.

Esther is one of three books in the Bible primarily about women—the book of Esther, the book of Ruth, and the Song of Solomon. Each book is a delightful and engaging love story on the surface—but each contains hidden treasures of meaning just beneath the surface, embedded in the form of types, symbols, and metaphors.

This precious and wonderful book has been the subject of much scholarly controversy down through the years. It has had its share of critics and even opponents. That great leader of the Reformation, Martin Luther, once complained, "The book of Esther I toss into the Elbe [River]. . . . I am such an enemy to the book of Esther that I wish it did not exist."[1] This statement shows that even a great reformer of the church can be stubbornly wrong about God's Word.

HER STORY IS OUR STORY

One of the most unusual features of the book of Esther is the fact that the name of God never appears in its pages (the only other book of the Bible that does not mention God by name is Song of Solomon). There is nothing about the story of Esther that is distinctly "religious"—that is, there is no reference to worship or faith, nor any prophecies of Christ, heaven, or hell. Many people wonder why this is so.

The answer, I believe, is that the story of Esther resonates with our own stories, our own experience—and in our own lives. It is often hard for us to see God at work. He often seems invisible and silent and uninvolved—yet, as the story of Esther clearly shows, even when we can't see Him, He is at work in our lives, arranging events and circumstances to accomplish His good and loving plan for our lives.

Queen Esther's story is our story. She was thrust into a time of great crisis and peril—both for herself and her people. She was called upon to demonstrate character qualities of courage and faithfulness. In order to save her people from destruction, she needed to risk everything, including her own life—not rashly or wantonly, but with wisdom, skill, and reliance on God.

You and I face tremendous challenges in our daily lives. We may not be called upon to save an entire culture from genocide—but we may be called upon to risk our finances, our security, our reputations, our friendships, and even our very lives to serve God and others at such a time as this.

What are the needs and the perils you see around you today? Maybe there are children at risk in your neighborhood, and they need someone to come to their aid and say, "God loves you, and I am here to help you." Maybe there are troubled youths or pregnant teens who have nowhere else to turn, and you sense God telling you, "I have placed you here for such a time as this." Perhaps you see your neighbors or your church or your community or even your nation entering a time of great crisis. You feel God tugging at your heart and whispering to your conscience—"Now is the time! I am calling you to stand in the gap for such a time as this."

You may think, "But how do I know if it's really God speaking to me? I can't see Him. I can't hear His voice. God seems distant, even absent." Exactly so! That's how Esther felt! Perhaps that's why God's name does not appear in the book—could it be that He wants us to see how His people should respond in times of crisis when He seems invisible and silent?

And as you read through the book of Esther, you will see that God is not absent. Invisible, yes; absent, no! His actions are on every page and in every line. He is not named in the story, but He is truly the Author and Prime Mover of the story.

And He is the Author and Prime Mover of your story and mine.

THE HISTORICAL CONTEXT

The events of the book of Esther take place in the royal courts of Susa, one of the oldest cities of the world. Susa was located about 150 miles east of the Tigris River. The Iranian town of Shush now occupies the site where the splendid royal city of Susa once thrived.

You may wonder how Esther and her fellow Jews came to be in Persia, so far from their homeland in Palestine. To answer that question, we must go back to 2 Kings 25. There we read that the army of Nebuchadnezzar, King of Babylon, surrounded Jerusalem and laid siege to the city. After a siege lasting a year and a half, the city ran out of food and the people began to starve. The Jews made a last stand against the besieging forces, but the

Babylonians were victorious. The invaders captured the city, destroyed the temple and the royal palace, and ransacked the city. They broke down the city walls, took everything of value from the city, and led the people of Jerusalem into exile in distant Babylon. These events occurred in 586 BC.

Almost fifty years later, in 537 BC, the Persian ruler Cyrus the Great conquered Babylonia. Cyrus gave the Jewish people permission to return to Jerusalem and rebuild the city (see 2 Chronicles 36:22–23 and Ezra 1:1–2). Many of the Jews returned to the Promised Land and rebuilt the city of Jerusalem and its walls (as recorded in the books of Ezra and Nehemiah).

But a number of Jews remained behind and settled in the Persian Empire. Their descendants, the Mizrahi Jews, still live in Iran to this day, practicing their Hebrew faith and traditions (including the Feast of Purim, which celebrates the story of Esther) in the midst of one of the most fiercely Islamic cultures in the world.

Now that we have examined the background of the book of Esther, I have a suggestion: Before you go on to the next chapter in this book, I'd encourage you to open your Bible and read through the book of Esther. It's a short book, about the length of one or two chapters in a standard novel. You can easily read the entire book of Esther in a single sitting—certainly in less than half an hour. I know you'll find it a fascinating and rewarding story.

After you've finished, pick up this book again, and let's explore the book of Esther together.

2

A PAIR OF QUEENS

Esther 1

*N*ow that you have read through the book of Esther, I'm sure you've found it to be an intriguing and fascinating story—a delightful tale of romantic love and palace intrigue. It's a page-turner—the kind of story you have to keep reading to find out what happens next.

But just beneath the surface of the story is *another* story. It's the story of how God works *behind the scenes* of our lives to accomplish His purposes. In the pages of the book of Esther, we see how God is able to bring about His will even through the cruel, sinful choices of evil people. God does not make anyone sin, yet He is able to weave sinful human choices into His good plan.

This is the same principle Joseph explained to his brothers when he forgave them for selling him into slavery: "You intended to harm me, but God intended it for good to accomplish what is now being done, the saving of many lives" (Genesis 50:20). God can transform all the events in our lives, even the sinful actions of others, into righteous blessings. That is the message of the book of Esther.

As the apostle Paul tells us in the New Testament, "Now these things happened to them as an example, and they were written for our instruction, upon whom the ends of the ages have come" (1 Corinthians 10:11 NASB). Applied to the book of Esther, this principle means that her story can be viewed as a parable that instructs us in the deep spiritual truths of God.

Now, in calling the book of Esther a "parable," I am not suggesting that these events didn't actually occur. The events in the book of Esther *did indeed take place*. This is a book of authentic history—not legend or myth.

But it is recorded in such a way that we can see it as an instructive parable of spiritual truths for our lives. The book of Esther is not only a well-told, gripping narrative of actual historical events but it is also a rich illustration of a series of great truths God wants us to apply to our lives.

This approach to Old Testament narratives may be new to you. Perhaps this is the first time you have ever seen theological truths and spiritual principles extracted from the stories and symbols of the Old Testament. But this approach truly makes the Old Testament live for us today. If you learn to read your Old Testament as an aid to understanding the New Testament, you'll discover that the Bible is a beautiful and living book that continually yields an endless supply of practical insights and timeless truths.

The story of Esther is not only a powerful romantic drama and not only an accurate historical record but it can also be seen as a meaningful and instructive parable. As such, we will study it as we would study any of the parables of Jesus in the New Testament.

The Lord's favorite method of teaching was to tell stories that illustrated a point. Those stories were called parables. The word *parable* means to "lay something alongside." A closely related word is *parallel,* meaning "lined up alongside," like parallel rows of trees or parallel parking spaces. When we examine a New Testament parable, we find parallels between the story and everyday reality. In the parable of the prodigal son, for example, the prodigal son is a parallel of people who become lost in sin, and the loving father is a parallel of God, our gracious heavenly Father. We will see similar parallels occurring throughout the book of Esther.

We could say (keeping in mind that we are using the word *parable* to describe true stories as well as the fictional ones Jesus told) that the first parable God ever gave to the human race was the story of the creation of Adam and Eve. In that historical event, God took a rib from the side of Adam, made a woman, and laid her alongside the man. As the man looked into the woman's face, he saw a reflection of his own character and nature. That has the elements of a parable!

I'm defining *parable,* then, as "a story that is designed to help you see yourself more clearly." It's like a mirror that reflects your own life back to you, so you can see your own reality from a new perspective. Just as a mirror enables you to see that your hair isn't combed or that there is a smudge on your nose, a parable enables you to see some aspect of your own life from the outside. A mirror doesn't show you your defects so you can feel bad about yourself but so you can correct those defects. The same is true of parables.

So, as we approach this book, we will look for the parable, the story behind the true story. As the book of Esther unfolds, we will see that this story is really *our* story. This drama truly reveals God at work in *our* lives.

TWO QUEENS AND A KING

The first two chapters of Esther set the stage for us and introduce the action of the story. The title I have chosen for our study of Esther 1 is "A Pair of Queens." That phrase, "a pair of queens," probably evokes a mental image of a poker hand, and you may think that I'm inadvertently confessing to a misspent youth, wasting time and money at a poker table. So I hasten to say: Not true!

Is there another game in which a pair of queens figures prominently? Of course there is: The game of chess. The queen is the most powerful figure on the chessboard. She is always subject to the king, and her job is to attack the king's enemies and defend the king from attack. Though the king is more important than the queen, the queen is by far the more powerful of the two.

At the beginning of every game of chess, there are always two queens on the board. In the same way, the book of Esther begins with two queens, Vashti and Esther. The entire book revolves around one of these two queens, Queen Esther. It's the story of the kingdom, ruled by a king—but the fate of an entire people rests on the actions of the queen.

The book of Esther begins with a description of a magnificent kingdom, the Persian Empire:

> This is what happened during the time of Xerxes, the Xerxes who ruled over 127 provinces stretching from India to Cush: At that time King Xerxes reigned from his royal throne in the citadel of

Susa, and in the third year of his reign he gave a banquet for all his nobles and officials. The military leaders of Persia and Media, the princes, and the nobles of the provinces were present.

For a full 180 days he displayed the vast wealth of his kingdom and the splendor and glory of his majesty. When these days were over, the king gave a banquet, lasting seven days, in the enclosed garden of the king's palace, for all the people from the least to the greatest, who were in the citadel of Susa. The garden had hangings of white and blue linen, fastened with cords of white linen and purple material to silver rings on marble pillars. There were couches of gold and silver on a mosaic pavement of porphyry, marble, mother-of-pearl and other costly stones. Wine was served in goblets of gold, each one different from the other, and the royal wine was abundant, in keeping with the king's liberality. By the king's command each guest was allowed to drink in his own way, for the king instructed all the wine stewards to serve each man what he wished.

Queen Vashti also gave a banquet for the women in the royal palace of King Xerxes (Esther 1:1–9).

THE KING AND THE KINGDOM

As we read through this story, we will allow it to become a mirror in which we see our own reflection. The king represents you and me. This is an important principle that God wants us to understand: Every person is a kingdom ruled by a king. Your body is your kingdom—and a marvelously intricate and complex kingdom it is!

If you have ever studied the intricacies of the human body, you know that it is a marvelous creation, wonderfully efficient and purposefully designed. Every individual cell, every capillary, every nerve fiber is an astoundingly intricate example of biological engineering. And ruling over the whole of this kingdom is the king—the human soul, with its faculties of mind, emotion, and will.

Whatever the king decrees, the kingdom carries out. Whatever the mind and the emotions and the will choose to do, the body obeys. If the king is sick or incapacitated or unbalanced, the kingdom is affected. The body acts only upon the impulses that proceed from the soul. Now, perhaps, you can see the aptness and applicability of this parable, the book of Esther.

Let's take the allegory a step further: A king without a queen has no hope of a successor. If a king dies without having married and fathering a child, he has no heir to inherit the kingdom. A king who dies without leaving an heir is a king who has lost his kingdom. In the wake of his death, the kingdom is thrown into chaos and disorder.

Many belief systems in the world today teach that a human being is nothing more than an intelligent animal, a temporary collection of molecules, doomed to death, decay, and oblivion. Francis Crick, the co-discoverer of the spiral-shaped DNA molecule, once said, "Your joys and your sorrows, your memories and your ambitions, your sense of personal identity and free will, are in fact no more than the behavior of a vast assembly of nerve cells and their assorted molecules."[1] And biochemist Jacques Monod, in his book *Chance and Necessity*, wrote, "Man knows at last that he is alone in the universe's unfeeling immensity, out of which he emerged only by chance."[2]

If these learned men are correct, then human beings die just like animals. If we are nothing more than nerve cells and molecules that emerged by chance, then there is nothing beyond death, no immortality, no heaven, no hell—only a blank oblivion.

Political systems have been built on this philosophy. Both the Nazis and the Communists believed that a human being is nothing more than an animal—that a human being can be bred like an animal, genetically improved like an animal, caged like an animal, starved like an animal, terrorized like an animal, and slaughtered like an animal. According to this philosophy, there is no moral obligation to treat a human being as anything but a dumb brute.

But God's Word teaches that human beings are more than animals. A human being is not just a collection of cells. God gave human beings a spirit as well as a soul. Some people confuse the spirit with the soul, thinking that the two are synonymous. But the soul and spirit are not the same.

The soul, as we have said, consists of the mind, the emotions, and the will. And the spirit is immortal. When the human body dies, the spirit does not perish but lives on eternally.

Here is one way to look at the two: If the soul is like the king that commands the kingdom of the body, then the spirit is like a queen. It's in the realm of the spirit that human beings find comfort and refreshment from God. It's in the realm of the spirit that human beings have fellowship with God. The king (the soul) goes to the queen (the spirit) for comfort and refreshing counsel. The spirit is where the soul goes to experience communion with God.

The story of Esther can be seen to describe beautifully the most intimate activity of human nature—that intimate and delicate communion of the soul and the spirit. There is only one thing that can expose that delicate union and bring it to light: the Word of God. As the Scriptures tell us, "For the word of God is living and active. Sharper than any double-edged sword, *it penetrates even to dividing soul and spirit*, joints and marrow; it judges the thoughts and attitudes of the heart" (Hebrews 4:12, emphasis added). God's Word, through the guidance of the Holy Spirit, can reach down to the very innermost recesses of our lives and unlock the deepest level of our conscious existence.

THE QUEEN'S REFUSAL— AND THE KING'S RAGE

We have already seen King Xerxes' arrogance and pride (v. 4). After making a six-months-long display of his wealth and splendor, he gives a huge weeklong party for all the people in his citadel. The theme of the party: "Look at me! I am so great!" Once the party is in full swing, with wine flowing like water, the drunken king issues a command—and we shall see that this king was not only prideful and self-important but also depraved:

> On the seventh day, when King Xerxes was in high spirits from wine, he commanded the seven eunuchs who served him—Mehuman, Biztha, Harbona, Bigtha, Abagtha, Zethar and Carcas—to bring before him Queen Vashti, wearing her royal crown, in order

to display her beauty to the people and nobles, for she was lovely to look at. But when the attendants delivered the king's command, Queen Vashti refused to come. Then the king became furious and burned with anger (Esther 1:10-12).

Here we see a drunken king who is totally degenerate in his thinking. The wine he has swilled exposes the lewd depths of his mind, and he seeks to degrade his wife, his queen. Though the text is somewhat ambiguous on this point, many Bible scholars believe that in this passage King Xerxes commands Queen Vashti to parade before his guests wearing *only* her crown. This interpretation would certainly explain why Queen Vashti took the extreme risk of refusing the king's command.

When the queen disobeyed, the king flew into a rage, and he immediately took counsel of his legal experts to determine how to deal with Queen Vashti's defiance:

> Since it was customary for the king to consult experts in matters of law and justice, he spoke with the wise men who understood the times and were closest to the king—Carshena, Shethar, Admatha, Tarshish, Meres, Marsena and Memucan, the seven nobles of Persia and Media who had special access to the king and were highest in the kingdom.
>
> "According to law, what must be done to Queen Vashti?" he asked. "She has not obeyed the command of King Xerxes that the eunuchs have taken to her."
>
> Then Memucan replied in the presence of the king and the nobles, "Queen Vashti has done wrong, not only against the king but also against all the nobles and the peoples of all the provinces of King Xerxes. For the queen's conduct will become known to all the women, and so they will despise their husbands and say, 'King Xerxes commanded Queen Vashti to be brought before him, but she would not come.' This very day the Persian and Median women of the nobility who have heard about the queen's conduct will respond to all the king's nobles in the same way. There will be no end of disrespect and discord.

"Therefore, if it pleases the king, let him issue a royal decree and let it be written in the laws of Persia and Media, which cannot be repealed, that Vashti is never again to enter the presence of King Xerxes. Also let the king give her royal position to someone else who is better than she. Then when the king's edict is proclaimed throughout all his vast realm, all the women will respect their husbands, from the least to the greatest."

The king and his nobles were pleased with this advice, so the king did as Memucan proposed. He sent dispatches to all parts of the kingdom, to each province in its own script and to each people in its own language, proclaiming in each people's tongue that every man should be ruler over his own household (Esther 1:13–22).

Here we have the story of a king who has tried to degrade and humiliate his own queen. When she refused his insulting, drunken command, the king cut himself off from her fellowship forever. What parallel to our lives can we find in the opening scene of this story?

YOU ARE A KING

When the story opens, we see that the kingdom is prosperous and at peace. There is no external threat to the empire of Xerxes. It's a time of peace, blessing, and fruitfulness throughout Persia. The king holds a half-year-long celebration to demonstrate his own glory, pomp, and majesty—and as a king, he symbolically represents the human soul, yours and mine.

Where do we get the idea that a human being is a king? It comes directly from God's own Word. David the Psalmist reveals a deep truth as he sings about the nature of our humanity:

When I consider your heavens,
the work of your fingers,
the moon and the stars,
which you have set in place,
What is man that you are mindful of him,
the son of man that you care for him?

24

You made him a little lower than the heavenly beings
  and crowned him with glory and honor.
You made him ruler over the works of your hands;
  you put everything under his feet (Psalm 8:3–6).

What is humanity? A ruler over the world God has made—but not by his own right. It is God who crowns humanity with glory and honor. It is God who gives us dominion.

When God created unfallen human beings, he intended each of us to be a king, properly governing both ourselves and our domain upon the earth. God intended for each of us to exercise godly dominion. In so doing, we would display the majesty, glory, and power of the God who created us and dwells in us. That is what humanity was intended to do.

We human beings have never forgotten that we are to exercise dominion. Our kingship is programmed into our souls and encoded in our DNA. Because of sin, that desire to exercise dominion has sometimes been twisted into a lust for power and control, like that of a conqueror or totalitarian dictator. But vestiges of the original, unfallen, godly desire for righteous dominion of the earth still remain.

What motivates human beings to climb Mount Everest? People spend small fortunes, invest months in training and preparation, undergo hardship, and risk their lives in order to reach "the top of the world." And what do they see when they get to the summit? Just the other side of the mountain.

Why do they do it? Because human beings have never forgotten that they were given dominion over all the earth. God created us to be bold, adventurous, curious, and persistent in our quest to master the forces, mysteries, and secrets of the world. Whenever we discover some new piece of knowledge about our universe, we display the glory of the God who indwells us.

That is our function as human beings. Humanity was made to glorify God. You are a king, and so am I. So it was with Adam in the Garden of Eden. Adam's purpose in life was to display, through his humanity, all the majesty, glory, and wisdom of the God who made him and indwelt him.

A PROUD AND FOOLISH KING

As we read this story in Esther, we find that Xerxes was not content to display only the authority that was properly his as king. As the party continued, as he reveled in the praise of all the people who were eating his food and drinking his wine, Xerxes became arrogant and proud. He believed that the glory and majesty that he had displayed were of his own making.

Puffed up with pride and made foolish by his excessive indulgence in wine, he perverted his own God-given kingship. In an act of self-centered hubris and arrogance, Xerxes sent for his queen, his own wife, and he gave her a humiliating command to come and display her beauty and glory before the drunken crowd.

Whenever a man is drunk, either with alcohol or with selfish pride, he invariably hurts the ones he loves. And this king was drunk with *both* alcohol and pride.

As a pastor, I have counseled many couples, and I've often found this to be the case: When we become proud and self-centered, the first thing we do is take it out on our loved ones. When we are offended by the boss or a co-worker at the office, we go home and snap at our families. Often, we treat our loved ones with a degree of contempt and insensitivity that we would never use against a stranger.

Why? Why do we degrade the very ones who deserve our deepest love and highest esteem? It's because that's the nature of sin.

When this king was lifted up in pride, he began to imagine that the glory of his kingship was all of his own making. In his pride, he sent a command to the woman who was rightfully reserved for his intimate and private communion. He told her to put herself on display for the amusement of his guests. He sought to make a mockery of her before them all.

But she refused his unrighteous command. And this king found that the queen would not let him take dominion over her dignity and self-esteem. There are limits to what even a king can do.

Let's apply this lesson to the story of humanity as we trace it through the Scriptures.

First, consider this question: When did humanity fall? When did Adam fall? Isn't it amazing that when we read the story of the so-called "Fall of Man" in Genesis 3, we see that it isn't a *man's* fall that is recorded, but the fall of a *woman*? Did Adam fall when Eve ate the fruit? No. Eve's fall was simply the way by which Satan found his way into Adam's life. Her fall was the channel by which the tempter approached the man.

Then when did Adam fall? He fell when he chose to assert the supremacy of his soul—his mind, emotions, and his will—over the revelation of truth that God had placed in the inner chambers of his spirit. Adam had known God on a face-to-face basis. God had revealed His truth to Adam through direct, face-to-face revelation.

After Eve fell, Adam tried to reverse the order of his own nature and to make his reason superior to the revelation he had received from God. Thus Adam downgraded the rightful function of his spirit. The king within Adam (his soul) issued an unrighteous command to the queen (his spirit). Yet even as Adam tried to do this, he found it impossible. A human being cannot change his or her own nature. We can tamper with the nature of the world, rearranging chemicals and wielding atomic forces—all of this is within our dominion. But it is impossible to change our own nature.

As we've seen, when Xerxes wrongfully summoned Queen Vashti, she refused his command. In a fit of prideful rage, the king made a choice from which he could never retreat. He chose to completely cut himself off from his queen.

When Eve approached Adam with the fruit of disobedience, he understood clearly what the issues were. He deliberately chose what his own reason told him while rejecting God's revelation. Adam ate of the fruit of disobedience—and he cut himself off from the glory of God in his own spirit. So he entered into the state of lonely restlessness that has characterized the human condition ever since.

FREE WILL AND CONSEQUENCES

Beginning at verse 13, we see a number of odd details introduced into the story. We learn that "it was customary for the king to consult experts in matters of law and justice," so the king consults with his wise men. "According to law," he asks, "what must be done to Queen Vashti? She has not obeyed the command of King Xerxes that the eunuchs have taken to her" (v. 15).

In other words: "What is to be done with this woman who refused to obey the king? What is to be done with this spirit who refuses to submit to my prideful soul?"

One of the king's wise men, named Memucan, replies that the queen's insubordination is upsetting the entire kingdom. He therefore recommends that the queen be punished: "Therefore, if it pleases the king, let him issue a royal decree and let it be written in the laws of Persia and Media, which cannot be repealed, that Vashti is never again to enter the presence of King Xerxes. Also let the king give her royal position to someone else who is better than she" (v. 19).

Once decreed, this law cannot be changed. By analogy, we can equate this to something Paul, in his letter to the Romans, calls the "law of sin and death" (8:2)—an unchangeable, irrevocable law. We know it in secular life as the law of retribution, or the law of inevitable consequence. We all have free will and the right to make moral choices. But choices always come with consequences. We have no power to revoke those consequences once the choice has been made.

Let's say that I have two glasses of clear liquid. One glass is labeled "water." The other is labeled "poison." I am thirsty, and I know that I can trust those labels. The one glass can quench my thirst, and the other will assuredly kill me. Now, I have a choice to make: I can drink the water, or I can drink the poison.

If I choose to drink the poison, I do so by my own free will. Once I have made my choice and have swallowed the poison, consequences will flow from that choice. I can no longer control those consequences. I cannot object that those consequences are unfair. In making my choice, I have set in motion a law that cannot be changed—the law of inevitable consequence.

In the Garden of Eden, when Adam chose to heed the voice of his reason over the voice of revelation, when he chose the desire of his own heart over fellowship with God, he set in motion a series of consequences that he was powerless to change. It was the law of sin and death.

At that point, the human spirit became dark and unresponsive. Humanity became a soulish race, governed by the mind, the emotions, and the will. The human ego sat upon the throne of the human kingdom, permitting no opposition. Human beings looked only to their own emotions and rationalizations for guidance in making decisions in life.

The prideful, egotistical rage of the King of Persia, unleashed against his wife, his queen, pictures for us the folly, injustice, and sin of the human life. This is the tragic story of Xerxes and Queen Vashti—and it is the tragic parable of Adam and Eve, and of your life and mine.

But of course the story does not end there. So far, we have met only one queen, and this is the story of two queens. The second and more important queen is about to take her place on the stage of this drama.

3

QUEEN ESTHER AND MORDECAI

Esther 2

From September 1940 through May 1941, Nazi Germany carried out hundreds of bombing raids over Britain, a campaign known as the Blitz. Even during the height of the Blitz, when London endured fifty-seven consecutive nights of bombing, the royal family of England remained close to London. King George VI and Queen Elizabeth stayed at Buckingham Palace while their daughters, Princess Elizabeth and Princess Margaret, were sent to Windsor Castle, just twenty miles from the heart of London and within easy reach of German bombers.

The future queen, Princess Elizabeth, was a teenager at the time. Her mother, when asked if Elizabeth and her younger sister Margaret would be evacuated to Canada, replied, "The children won't go without me. I won't leave without the King. And the King will never leave." In this way, the royal family stood shoulder to shoulder with the British people during England's darkest hour.

After her eighteenth birthday, Princess Elizabeth joined the Auxiliary Territorial Service, where she was known as No. 230873 Second Sub-altern Elizabeth Windsor. She worked as a driver and truck mechanic, achieving the rank of Junior Commander. On one occasion, her father, King George VI, visited her in the motor pool. He found her dressed in overalls, working under the hood of a military vehicle, with grease all over her hands, clothing, and face. He watched her for a while as she tried in vain to start the engine.

"What? You haven't got it going yet?" he said, grinning.

31

"No," the future queen said. "I can't figure out what's wrong!"

The king walked away, still grinning. In his hands was the distributor cap he had removed from the engine while his daughter wasn't looking.[1]

Perilous times demand much from a princess—and from a queen.

ENTER MORDECAI

Chapter 1 of the book of Esther set the stage and drew back the curtain on a dramatic scene of a king's pride and rage, which led to the vindictive banishment of the queen. In contrast to chapter 1, chapter 2 presents a scene of redeeming grace. We read:

> Later when the anger of King Xerxes had subsided, he remembered Vashti and what she had done and what he had decreed about her. Then the king's personal attendants proposed, "Let a search be made for beautiful young virgins for the king. Let the king appoint commissioners in every province of his realm to bring all these beautiful girls into the harem at the citadel of Susa. Let them be placed under the care of Hegai, the king's eunuch, who is in charge of the women; and let beauty treatments be given to them. Then let the girl who pleases the king be queen instead of Vashti." This advice appealed to the king, and he followed it (Esther 2:1–4).

As this scene opens, we see the king, Xerxes, vainly seeking to satisfy his restless soul and fill the vacuum in his life. His anger has subsided, and he realizes what he has done. He has banished his wife, his queen—and now he must face the emptiness and loneliness of living alone in that huge royal citadel.

Here we see a picture of what a human life looks like without God—restless, lonely, dissatisfied, constantly seeking, never finding. Such people do not dare to be alone with their own thoughts. They are constantly looking for something to anesthetize the pain of loneliness. So they seek diversion through a never-ending quest for thrills, pleasure, entertainment, or conquest. That is the story of humanity.

In the next few verses we are introduced to the two most important characters in this story:

> Now there was in the citadel of Susa a Jew of the tribe of Benjamin, named Mordecai son of Jair, the son of Shimei, the son of Kish, who had been carried into exile from Jerusalem by Nebuchadnezzar king of Babylon, among those taken captive with Jehoiachin king of Judah. Mordecai had a cousin named Hadassah, whom he had brought up because she had neither father nor mother. This girl, who was also known as Esther, was lovely in form and features, and Mordecai had taken her as his own daughter when her father and mother died (Esther 2:5–7).

Mordecai is a pivotal figure in this drama. A man of great wisdom and a keen tactical thinker, he served as Esther's adoptive father, advisor, mentor, and conscience. Mordecai was a Jew of the tribe of Benjamin. As a member of the Hebrew race, he served as one of God's chosen agents, and God used him in a mighty way to change the course of human history. Down through the centuries, God has always used His chosen people, the Jews, in such strategic ways.

The origin of the name *Mordecai* is uncertain. Some experts suggest that it may have come from a Hebrew root word meaning "bitter" or "bruising." Certainly, the plight of the Hebrew people while in captivity was a bitter and bruising experience; perhaps the Spirit of God chose a man so named to remind us, down through the ages, of what the Jewish people went through while in exile. Others have suggested that the name is derived from an Aramaic term used to address an honored gentlemen, a term meaning "one who attains merit or favor." Mordecai certainly displays great personal merit, ingenuity, wisdom, and faith in the course of these events.

Some experts believe the name *Mordecai* is the Hebrew form of a Persian word meaning, "little man;" that is, a man who has humbled himself. I lean toward this interpretation because I believe that Mordecai symbolizes Jesus, the One who humbled himself and became a man, who set aside His glory and entered human life, becoming one of us and choosing to be obedient unto death, even the death of the cross (see Philippians 2:5–8).

Symbols in Scripture often represent more than one great truth. As we trace the character of Mordecai through this story, it's easy to recognize him as a symbol not only of Jesus but also of the Holy Spirit. The Spirit's task is to exalt Jesus, the One who came to redeem fallen humanity, and to restore human beings to that intimate fellowship with God that was lost at the fall. We will find Mordecai symbolizing the activity of the Spirit throughout this story.

ENTER THE NEW QUEEN

In this passage, we also meet the new queen, Esther. As we discussed in the previous chapter, the queen symbolizes the human spirit, which is part of our human makeup. Vashti, the first queen, represented the unregenerate human spirit; Esther, the second queen, represents the redeemed and regenerate human spirit after conversion.

The spirit and the soul are two distinct components of the human personality. The human soul is lonely and restless when estranged from the spirit, just as Xerxes was lonely and restless when he was estranged from Vashti, his first queen.

Esther's Hebrew name is *Hadassah,* which means "myrtle," a lowly shrub commonly regarded as the symbol of the nation of Israel. Many scholars believe the Persian name *Esther* means "star," but noted Bible scholar Wilhelm Gesenius (1786–1842), said that the name *Esther* derives from a word meaning "to hide" or "hidden," which is a beautiful description not only of Esther's hidden status as a Jew among Gentiles but also of the hidden status of the spirit of man.

Mordecai begins at once to bring Esther and the king together:

> When the king's order and edict had been proclaimed, many girls were brought to the citadel of Susa and put under the care of Hegai. Esther also was taken to the king's palace and entrusted to Hegai, who had charge of the harem. The girl pleased him and won his favor. Immediately he provided her with her beauty treatments and special food. He assigned to her seven maids selected from the king's palace and moved her and her maids into the best place in the harem.

Esther had not revealed her nationality and family background, because Mordecai had forbidden her to do so. Every day he walked back and forth near the courtyard of the harem to find out how Esther was and what was happening to her (Esther 2:8–11).

Mordecai (symbolizing the Holy Spirit) managed to place Esther in the line of the king's search. Here we can see a parallel to the way the Holy Spirit arranges circumstances in human lives to achieve God's purposes. Throughout the Bible, we see again and again how God seeks out human beings, while those same human beings think all the while that they have been seeking God.

The Bible contains many exhortations such as, "Seek the LORD while he may be found; call on him while he is near" (Isaiah 55:6), and "He is a rewarder of them that diligently seek him," (Hebrews 11:6 KJV). So we seek after God, and we find Him. At the end of our search, though, we are astounded to discover that it was God who sought us all along.

In the same way, the account in Esther provides a clear example of the old saying, "He pursued her until she caught him." King Xerxes searched the entire kingdom for a bride. Yet, at the end of his search, it was clear that Esther, guided by Mordecai, came to the throne through strategies and maneuvers that Xerxes couldn't even imagine.

In one sense, this Gentile king had no right to marry Esther. She belonged to a special race, the chosen people of God. Jews were forbidden by God's law to marry with another race. She was a Jew—yet she was here in this foreign land. The sovereign, overruling grace of God placed her within the scope of the king's search. When Xerxes saw her, he knew she was the one for whom his heart yearned. Although Xerxes had no legal right to marry a woman of the Jewish race, God was gracious to the king so that His plan for the Jewish people could be fulfilled through Esther.

God's grace to Xerxes symbolizes His grace to us all. You and I have no right to a redeemed spirit. Someone has well said, "The only right human beings have is the right to be damned." If we insist upon our right to be condemned forever, then that is what we shall receive. But God in His grace has overruled our right to eternal damnation. He has placed within the scope of our search the very thing for which we are searching.

When our spirits are made alive by grace through faith in Jesus Christ, we discover that a redeemed spirit is the one thing we have been yearning for. We find that Jesus is the One who satisfies the hunger of our souls.

THE CONVERSION OF THE KING

Finally, it is Esther's turn to be brought before the king. We read:

> Before a girl's turn came to go in to King Xerxes, she had to complete twelve months of beauty treatments prescribed for the women, six months with oil of myrrh and six with perfumes and cosmetics. And this is how she would go to the king: Anything she wanted was given her to take with her from the harem to the king's palace. In the evening she would go there and in the morning return to another part of the harem to the care of Shaashgaz, the king's eunuch who was in charge of the concubines. She would not return to the king unless he was pleased with her and summoned her by name.
>
> When the turn came for Esther (the girl Mordecai had adopted, the daughter of his uncle Abihail) to go to the king, she asked for nothing other than what Hegai, the king's eunuch who was in charge of the harem, suggested. And Esther won the favor of everyone who saw her. She was taken to King Xerxes in the royal residence in the tenth month, the month of Tebeth, in the seventh year of his reign.
>
> Now the king was attracted to Esther more than to any of the other women, and she won his favor and approval more than any of the other virgins. So he set a royal crown on her head and made her queen instead of Vashti. And the king gave a great banquet, Esther's banquet, for all his nobles and officials. He proclaimed a holiday throughout the provinces and distributed gifts with royal liberality (Esther 2:12–18).

I believe that this passage describes a "conversion" of sorts for King Xerxes. Esther immediately won the king's favor, and he immediately recognized in her the answer to the emptiness and restlessness of his life.

So he set a symbol of royalty upon her head, granted her authority in his kingdom, and found the beginning of a new life. Throughout the kingdom there was an immediate effect: A lifting of the heavy burden of taxation plus the gracious distribution of royal gifts.

This scene can be taken as a symbol of what the New Testament means when it says, "Therefore, if anyone is in Christ, he is a new creation; the old has gone, the new has come!" (2 Corinthians 5:17). At conversion, life begins anew. The burden and guilt of sin are lifted, and we receive royal gifts of blessing from God. As the hymn writer George W. Robinson (1838–1877) wrote:

> Heav'n above is softer blue,
> Earth around is sweeter green!
> Something lives in every hue
> Christless eyes have never seen;
> Birds with gladder songs o'erflow,
> flowers with deeper beauties shine,
> Since I know, as I now know,
> I am His, and He is mine.

When Christ enters our hearts, life begins anew.

THE PLOT AGAINST THE KING

Next, we see God's grace at work in the life of Xerxes. Mordecai and Esther have come into the life of this king—and God uses them to deliver Xerxes from a plot that threatens his life.

When the virgins were assembled a second time, Mordecai was sitting at the king's gate. But Esther had kept secret her family background and nationality just as Mordecai had told her to do, for she continued to follow Mordecai's instructions as she had done when he was bringing her up.

During the time Mordecai was sitting at the king's gate, Bigthana and Teresh, two of the king's officers who guarded the doorway, became angry and conspired to assassinate King Xerxes. But

Mordecai found out about the plot and told Queen Esther, who in turn reported it to the king, giving credit to Mordecai. And when the report was investigated and found to be true, the two officials were hanged on a gallows. All this was recorded in the book of the annals in the presence of the king (Esther 2:19–23).

The life of the king is threatened. This threat can be seen to symbolize the existence of an evil force that is at work to destroy humanity, to capture the human mind, emotions, and will. This evil force, which we know as Satan, seeks to pervert human beings to its own use and to oppose God's purpose in human lives.

This same evil force is at work in your own life—your own kingdom. The life of the "king" within you is threatened. Your soul is the prize in this great spiritual battle, which is waged within the soul of every human being.

When the enemy of King Xerxes tries to strike, Mordecai learns of the plot. He is seated in the gate as a judge in the city, but he does not have access to the palace, so he reports the plot to Queen Esther. She, in turn, reports the plot to the king, giving credit to Mordecai.

Xerxes investigates, discovers the report of the plot is true, and orders the conspirators taken out and publicly "hanged on a gallows." If you think that these two conspirators were hanged with a rope around their necks, you have a mistaken impression. In the original Hebrew language, this phrase refers to being nailed to, or impaled upon, a tree or post. Such a description can remind us of the crucifixion of Jesus Christ. In Colossians we read:

> When you were dead in your sins and in the uncircumcision of your sinful nature, God made you alive with Christ. He forgave us all our sins, having canceled the written code, with its regulations, that was against us and that stood opposed to us; he took it away, nailing it to the cross. And having disarmed the powers and authorities, he made a public spectacle of them, triumphing over them by the cross (Colossians 2:13–15).

The evil force in our lives that threatens to overcome us was defeated at the cross—just as the threats to King Xerxes were defeated "on a gallows." This graphic Old Testament account can serve to remind us that our enemy's doom is certain. His plan will not prevail.

Notice this concluding statement: "All this was recorded in the book of the annals in the presence of the king." In a similar way, God has recorded what He has done for us in a book. When we begin to understand what that book says about the deliverance He has purchased for us through the death of His Son and when we realize that our enemy has been nailed to the tree as a public example, we will begin to experience the deliverance God intends for our lives.

If you have ever lived apart from Christ, then you know what it means to wander in a wilderness of loneliness and restlessness. You know what it means to search in vain for something to satisfy your soul. Having tried everything and having found nothing, you came at last to realize that only Jesus could satisfy the deep need of your heart. Today, you look back with gratitude to that wonderful moment of conversion. You look forward with eager expectation to the fulfillment of His promise when you will be with Him in glory.

But what about that period of time in between? Conversion is just the beginning of the story. Did you think this was all there was to the Christian life? There is so much more to your story and mine—and there is so much more to the story of Esther. These first chapters merely set the stage for the deliverance God intends to work in the life of the king of this kingdom.

And conversion merely sets the stage for the work of deliverance He seeks to accomplish in your life and mine—and the kingdoms of our own hearts. As we continue exploring the story of Esther, we'll discover what God wants to do in every human life in whom Jesus Christ has found a throne. He will expose to us the hidden plot against our lives—the satanic scheme that seeks to keep us in bondage to our own selfish ways.

Once our eyes are opened to the threat we face, we'll know to turn to the One who took our sins upon himself on the cross. Then our Lord will bring us into that glorious place of liberty and freedom reserved for all who are called the "sons of God" (Galatians 3:26).

4

POWER STRUGGLE

Esther 3

*I*n Iran's Kermanshah Province, near the town of Jeyhounabad, there is a great rock called Mount Behistun. The face of the rock has been sheared off, forming a towering limestone cliff. Carved into that rock, some 300 feet above the base of the cliff, is a series of images and an inscription in three ancient cuneiform languages—Old Persian, Elamite, and Babylonian. The images depict the ancient Persian king Darius the Great, archer's bow in hand, with his foot on the chest of a conquered enemy. The inscription describes the glory of Darius' reign.

Darius the Great was a descendant of Cyrus the Great, who ruled over the kingdoms of Persia and Media. Cyrus the Great was the Persian king who gave the exiled Jews their freedom and issued a decree that the Jews be permitted to return to their homeland and rebuild the city of Jerusalem (2 Chronicles 36:22).

Darius the Great was succeeded on the Persian throne by a king known as Xerxes, or Ahasuerus, who ruled Persia from 486 to 465 BC. It was this king who banished Queen Vashti and married a young Jewish woman called Hadassah or Queen Esther.

The events we read about in the book of Esther, the book of Nehemiah, and other Old Testament books are confirmed by archaeological records. Secular history and biblical history are inextricably intertwined. The Old Testament accounts are not legends or myths. These are reliable historical documents.

But as we have already seen, the story of Esther is important not merely as an incident out of history. It is also important because these events can be seen to represent spiritual principles that affect us all.

By way of analogy, you are the king of your own kingdom. The empire of your life reaches out and has an impact on all who come in contact with you. If you are a Christian, then you found a new "queen" when your spirit was made alive in Jesus Christ. You became aware of the influence of the Holy Spirit, who has recorded in a book the story of an evil plot against your life. This is how the story of Esther retraces the story of your life.

We have reached the place in the book of Esther that represents everything that most believers know about the Christian life. Many Christians, who have accepted Christ and know they are born again, feel that they have been left here to struggle along and make the most of this life until the Lord either calls them home through death or comes for them in the clouds. Meanwhile, they are stuck on earth, trying hard to make the best of a bad situation in this fallen world.

If that was the sum total of the Christian life, then our lessons from the book of Esther would end at chapter 2. But the story doesn't end there. It goes on to teach some profoundly important truths, as we will discover in Esther 3.

HAMAN THE AGAGITE

I once had a conversation with the wife of a Protestant minister. She told me that her husband had faithfully preached the gospel of Jesus Christ throughout his ministry. Again and again, he preached that Jesus Christ died to save men and women from sin. He ended every sermon with an invitation for people to come forward, receive Christ as Lord and Savior, and begin to live a new life in Him.

But, she said, his ministry was falling apart and his home was breaking up. Why? Because, while he had focused on what the Word of God says about the *beginning* of the Christian life, he had ignored everything the Word of God says about life *after* conversion. He had failed to live according to the principles and standards the Lord set for all of those who follow Him.

POWER STRUGGLE (*Esther 3*)

In Esther 3 and beyond, the richly meaningful story of Queen Esther can show us how we are to live following conversion. Her life unveils for us the activity of evil in our lives—and how God works to deliver us from the evil that plots against us. We pick up the story of Queen Esther with the opening lines of chapter 3:

> After these events, King Xerxes honored Haman son of Hamme-datha, the Agagite, elevating him and giving him a seat of honor higher than that of all the other nobles. All the royal officials at the king's gate knelt down and paid honor to Haman, for the king had commanded this concerning him. But Mordecai would not kneel down or pay him honor.
>
> Then the royal officials at the king's gate asked Mordecai, "Why do you disobey the king's command?" Day after day they spoke to him but he refused to comply. Therefore they told Haman about it to see whether Mordecai's behavior would be tolerated, for he had told them he was a Jew.
>
> When Haman saw that Mordecai would not kneel down or pay him honor, he was enraged. Yet having learned who Mordecai's people were, he scorned the idea of killing only Mordecai. Instead Haman looked for a way to destroy all Mordecai's people, the Jews, throughout the whole kingdom of Xerxes (Esther 3:1–6).

This passage introduces a new character—a villainous antagonist named Haman. We immediately see an antagonism between Mordecai and Haman. Why? What is the grievance that fuels the antipathy between them? We find a clue in the parentage of this man. He is called Haman, the son of Hamme-datha, the Agagite. You may well wonder: What is an Agagite?

Here we need to do a little detective work—and if you've never learned the thrill of "sleuthing the truth" of the Bible as if you were Sherlock Holmes, then you've missed one of the truly satisfying experiences of the Christian life. It's fascinating to pick up clues, to put puzzle pieces together, to find meaning and patterns in the tantalizing details we find in Scripture. The details in the background of Haman are highly intriguing.

Haman is an Agagite, a descendant of a man named Agag. Where do you find Agag in Scripture? In 1 Samuel 15. There we read that the prophet Samuel told Saul, the first king of Israel, to go to war against the Amalekites. We read:

> Samuel said to Saul, "I am the one the LORD sent to anoint you king over his people Israel; so listen now to the message from the LORD. This is what the LORD Almighty says: 'I will punish the Amalekites for what they did to Israel when they waylaid them as they came up from Egypt. Now go, attack the Amalekites and totally destroy everything that belongs to them. Do not spare them; put to death men and women, children and infants, cattle and sheep, camels and donkeys'" (1 Samuel 15:1–3).

So Saul gathered the people and went to battle, as the account continues:

> He took Agag king of the Amalekites alive, and all his people he totally destroyed with the sword. But Saul and the army spared Agag and the best of the sheep and cattle, the fat calves and lambs— everything that was good. These they were unwilling to destroy completely, but everything that was despised and weak they totally destroyed (1 Samuel 15:8–9).

Saul obeyed God—but only part-way. The Lord had told him to destroy the Amalekites totally—both the people and all of their herds. But Saul decided he knew better than the Lord. He showed clemency to Agag, the Amalekite king, and greedily spared the best of the Amalekite herds in violation of the Lord's command. Because of Saul's failure to obey, God sent Samuel the prophet to tell Saul that the kingdom would be taken from him and given to another.

Who were these Amalekites? Tracing their story back in time, we see that Amalek was the enemy of Israel when God's people came through the wilderness on the way from Egypt into Canaan. Exodus 17 contains the account of a great battle between Israel and the Amalekites. There we find the famous scene in which Moses, aided by Aaron and Hur, stands on the top of a hill with the rod of the Lord raised in his hand while Joshua leads the army of Israel in battle below. Whenever Moses' arms grow tired and he can no longer hold the rod aloft, the Amalekites begin to prevail. So Aaron and Hur help by adding their strength, raising Moses' arms higher. In the end, Joshua and his army prevail over the Amalekites.

Going back even farther we find that Amalek, the father of the Amalekite tribe, was the grandson of Jacob's son, Esau (see Genesis 36:12). All through the Bible, Amalek, Agag, and the descendants of Esau picture for us an enemy that is opposed to all that God would do.

So this is the history of Amalek and Agag that underlies the Haman's hostility toward Mordecai and the Jewish people. Mordecai refuses to pay honor to this Agagite, and Haman is enraged—not only by Mordecai's lack of respect but also by the fact that Mordecai is a member of the hated Jewish race, the historic enemies of the Amalekites. So Haman decides to take out his revenge not only against Mordecai but also against all of the Jewish people.

THE ENEMY WITHIN

As we have seen, the story of Esther symbolizes principles that are at work in every human heart. In the kingdom over which you reign, the kingdom of your own life, there is a Haman the Agagite. In the New Testament, this Haman-like principle is called "the flesh" (2 Peter 2:10), or as the NIV translates it, "the sinful nature." The flesh lives to exalt itself and continually seeks status and position in the eyes of other people. The flesh is never satisfied unless other people are bowing and scraping in front of it.

The flesh appears to us as a trusted friend, just as Haman appeared to King Xerxes—pretending to be a trusted advisor with only the king's best interests at heart. Yet Haman's true purpose was to advance himself and to force everyone to bow low before him. In our own lives, we often treat this traitor—the flesh—as if he were a friend. We promote him and advance him and give him a place of honor in our lives.

We know that pride is a sin, yet sometimes instead of being ashamed of our sinful pride, we boast of it, we trust in it, we regard pride as essential to life. Yet our fleshly pride is the Haman who lurks in our lives, pretending friendship while undermining all that is good and godly.

But just as Haman faced an implacable enemy in Mordecai, so the flesh faces an implacable foe in the life of a Christian. The "Mordecai" in our lives is the Holy Spirit. As Paul wrote, "For the sinful nature [literally, the flesh] desires what is contrary to the Spirit, and the Spirit what is contrary to the sinful nature. They are in conflict with each other," (Galatians 5:17). There never can be peace between Haman and Mordecai, between the flesh and the Spirit, because just as God has said that He will make war against Amalek from generation to generation, so He will never make peace with the flesh.

"Those controlled by the sinful nature [the flesh] cannot please God," Paul writes in Romans 8:8. The flesh is inherently displeasing to God, no matter how good the flesh may appear to us. God has sworn eternal enmity against our fleshly sin nature.

But that is not the end of the story. The Holy Spirit has landed like an invading force in the Christian heart. He has taken a beachhead in your life and mine, and He is steadily advancing and taking ground against the Haman-like enemy within us. He has come so that we might be delivered from the traitorous fiend, the Haman within. That is the spiritual principle pictured for us in the story of Haman, Mordecai, and King Xerxes.

Although the Spirit is advancing against the enemy, the war is not over. It has just begun. The Haman-like enemy, the flesh, is enraged by the mere presence of the Spirit. The flesh explodes in fury—and launches a counter-attack.

You may have experienced such a counterattack in your own life. You may have discovered that soon after you became a Christian you began to experience more trouble in your life than ever before. In your pre-Christian days, life went along fairly smoothly. But the moment you committed your life to Christ, you found yourself on a battleground. You felt yourself being torn in several directions at once. The Spirit within you was at war with your flesh—your sinful nature.

The flesh is not your friend but a subtle and crafty enemy. Therefore, it is vitally important that you learn to recognize the schemes and tactics of this enemy. You cannot experience victory unless you know your enemy and his ways. As Paul wrote, "For we are not unaware of his schemes" (2 Corinthians 2:11). If we know how our enemy works, we can call upon the conquering power of Jesus Christ to defeat him.

THE PEOPLE OF MORDECAI

Haman is enraged with Mordecai and now plans to destroy both Mordecai and his people. The next few verses detail for us Haman's strategy of death:

> In the twelfth year of King Xerxes, in the first month, the month of Nisan, they cast the *pur* (that is, the lot) in the presence of Haman to select a day and month. And the lot fell on the twelfth month, the month of Adar.
>
> Then Haman said to King Xerxes, "There is a certain people dispersed and scattered among the peoples in all the provinces of your kingdom whose customs are different from those of all other people and who do not obey the king's laws; it is not in the king's best interest to tolerate them. If it pleases the king, let a decree be issued to destroy them, and I will put ten thousand talents of silver into the royal treasury for the men who carry out this business" (Esther 3:7–9).

Haman is determined to manipulate the king and use the king to do his bidding. But Haman must achieve his goals without arousing the king's suspicions. So he approaches King Xerxes with great subtlety. This, of course, is how the Haman within each of us always tries to manipulate us.

It's hard to imagine how any Christian would succumb to a direct attack in which the flesh says to us, "Just reject God and live any way you please! Don't bother obeying Him any longer!" Such an assault would never work. We would instantly recognize the words of an enemy and reject them. The tempter never attacks so directly and brazenly. He always attacks with suggestions, questions, and other indirect means. In the same way, Haman begins in a roundabout way, not attacking Mordecai directly, but slyly attacking Mordecai's people, the Jews.

In the Bible, the story of the Jews is the story of God at work within humanity and human history. The whole purpose of this unique nation—the Jewish people—is that, in their history, we might see the evidence of God at work.

What do the Jewish people symbolize in this story for your life and mine? What gives evidence to the world that God is at work in your life? You will find a list of such evidences in Galatians 5:22–23: "But the fruit of the Spirit is love, joy, peace, patience, kindness, goodness, faithfulness, gentleness and self-control. Against such things there is no law." These are the evidences by which the world knows that the Spirit of God is at work in your life. The world is not fooled by some outward manifestation of miracles or other gifts. People in the world are looking for the manifestation of the fruit of the Spirit, the character qualities that reveal the character of God.

The fruit of the Spirit are the "people of Mordecai" in your life and mine.

THE SCHEMES OF HAMAN

The strategy of the flesh seeks to convince us that God's work in our lives is not to our advantage and that the fleshly strategies actually pay off. The flesh wants us to distrust God and reject His will for our lives, so that we will frustrate the work of the Holy Spirit in our lives. Haman knows this, so he goes after "the people of Mordecai."

To accomplish his aim, Haman brings another weapon to bear—the weapon of superstition. That's why we read that "they cast the *pur* (that is, the lot) in the presence of Haman to select a day and month." They cast lots to determine the lucky and propitious day for exterminating the Jews. Casting lots—a practice similar to shooting dice—was a common practice in oriental kingdoms. According to the lots they cast, the best day would be during the twelfth month, the month of Adar.

And there is more to Haman's plot. First, he tells the king that the Jewish people are scattered and dispersed throughout his kingdom, that they follow foreign laws, and that they do not keep the laws of the king of Persia. Then, after sowing seeds of distrust against the Jews in the king's mind,

Haman reveals his goal to the king: He wants nothing less than the complete destruction of the Jewish people. "If it pleases the king," Haman says, "let a decree be issued to destroy them, and I will put ten thousand talents of silver into the royal treasury for the men who carry out this business."

Notice Haman's blunt appeal to the king's greed. If the king agrees to Haman's plan, Haman will pay ten thousand silver talents—the equivalent of roughly $10 million in today's terms—into the king's treasury. Haman has openly suggested that Mordecai's people, the Jews, are unprofitable to the king. Destroy them, Haman says, and I will enrich the king's treasury by a staggering sum.

So Haman played on the two worst impulses of the king—his fear and his greed. He portrayed the Jewish people as a threat to the king's throne by claiming that the Jewish people did not obey the laws of the king of Persia (3:8). There is nothing more frightening to a king than a threat to the safety and security of his throne. Haman offered the king a way of making his throne more secure while also enriching the treasury. Haman knew exactly what to say in order to manipulate the king.

We must never forget that we all have a "Haman" within. Has Haman been talking to you recently? Has he tried to break your trust-relationship with God by appealing to your fears—or your greed? Perhaps you have seen that it is the people who break God's laws and live according to the flesh who always seem to advance in life. Haman may be whispering to you, "Why do you insist on being honest in all your dealings? What has your integrity ever gotten you? A little religion is fine on Sunday mornings, but on Monday through Friday, it's a dog-eat-dog out there—and honest guys finish last."

Has Haman been trying to manipulate and control the king within you? Have you begun to listen to his sweet, reasonable-sounding words? I urge you to turn Haman away while there is still time. Don't fall for his schemes.

FROM DECISION TO DELUSION

Haman is pursuing a program designed to defeat his enemies by manipulating and controlling the king. Haman's program begins with a *decision*:

> So the king took his signet ring from his finger and gave it to Haman son of Hammedatha, the Agagite, the enemy of the Jews. "Keep the money," the king said to Haman, "and do with the people as you please" (Esther 3:10–11).

Sin always begins with a decision. It is a decision to yield to temptation. Every action begins with the consent of the will. You have the final responsibility for everything you do, because everything you do begins with a decision. You may be perfectly sincere and confident that you are doing the right thing, just as King Xerxes was, but no evil enters your heart unless you have permitted it to be there by an act of your will.

Once you make a decision, you hand authority over to someone else. If you decide to resist temptation, then you hand authority over to the Holy Spirit. But if you decide to yield to temptation, then you hand authority over to the flesh. Once you decide, the power to act passes to either the Spirit of God or to the flesh.

Once the king made his decision to hand authority over to Haman, forces were set in motion that were beyond even the king's ability to control.

> Then on the thirteenth day of the first month the royal secretaries were summoned. They wrote out in the script of each province and in the language of each people all Haman's orders to the king's satraps, the governors of the various provinces and the nobles of the various peoples. These were written in the name of King Xerxes himself and sealed with his own ring. Dispatches were sent by couriers to all the king's provinces with the order to destroy, kill and annihilate all the Jews—young and old, women and little children—on a single day, the thirteenth day of the twelfth month, the month of Adar, and to plunder their goods. A copy of the text of the edict was to be issued as law in every province and made known to the people of every nationality so they would be ready for that day.
>
> Spurred on by the king's command, the couriers went out, and the edict was issued in the citadel of Susa (Esther 3:12–15).

Rarely does a moral decision affect only the person who makes it. What you decide in the depths of your heart affects everyone around you.

Every decision you make reaches out to the uttermost limits of your personal empire. Your secret thoughts become evident sooner or later. The entire kingdom is involved in all that the king does!

Haman's plan begins with *decision* and ends with *delusion*:

> The king and Haman sat down to drink, but the city of Susa was bewildered (Esther 3:15).

The king is falsely confident that he has taken a wise step. He is deluded, thinking he is acting in his own interest and the interests of the kingdom. Even though Haman has deceived him, manipulated him, and used him, King Xerxes is grateful for Haman's professed concern for the king's welfare. So the king invites Haman to celebrate with him with a glass of wine (or two or three).

Throughout the city, however, there is nothing but confusion and perplexity. To any reasonable citizen of the land, the king's edict seems monstrous and morally outrageous. To the citizens, the king of Persia seems to have taken leave of his senses. No one knows what to do. This strange genocidal edict has thrown the people into a state of bewilderment.

Upon a little reflection, you may be able to identify with the king at this point. There have undoubtedly been times in your life when you thought you were quite clever. You thought you had solved some major problem in your life, perhaps by cutting ethical corners or compromising your integrity. You got what you wanted, so you went home and patted yourself on the back.

That moment of celebration is what the king felt as he and Haman sat and shared a few drinks. The king believed Haman's claim that the Jewish people were a threat to his rule. Now he believed he had succeeded in removing that threat. He thought he had won.

But the king had merely allowed himself to be duped and exploited. Worse still, he had stirred up trouble in the populace. All the people of the city, who once thought him a wise and thoughtful ruler, were now perplexed by the obvious injustice of his order. King Xerxes was deluded into thinking he had made his kingdom safer. By listening to Haman and carrying out the Agagite's sly advice, he had spread resentment and ill will throughout his kingdom. He had put his own throne at risk.

We read in the book of Matthew that the Lord Jesus said, "The eye is the lamp of the body. If your eyes are good, your whole body will be full of light. But if your eyes are bad, your whole body will be full of darkness. If then the light within you is darkness, how great is that darkness!" (6:22–23). We often choose to live in darkness and delusion, listening to the treacherous advice of Haman instead of the wise counsel of the Holy Spirit.

The Spirit has come to open our eyes, the lamp of our bodies, so that our entire being can be filled with light. When we make a decision to trust what he tells us about our inner "Haman," the fleshly sinful nature, we allow Him to shine His life into our lives and chase away our bewilderment and confusion.

God does not leave us to wander blindly. He has shown the light of truth into our lives. As Jesus himself said to those Jews who believed in Him, "If you hold to my teaching, you are really my disciples. Then you will know the truth, and the truth will set you free" (John 8:31–32).

If you decide to believe what Haman tells you about God, you will wander in darkness and delusion. But if you believe what God tells you about the corrupt counsel of the flesh, your life will be filled with light and truth.

5

GOOD GRIEF!

Esther 4

*W*hat is the number one cause of weakness in the Christian life?
I submit to you that those who feel weak and powerless as Christians are not guilty of *deliberately* disobeying God. They are not *intentionally* doing what they *know* is wrong. Rather, they *want* to do right and they *try* to do right, yet they stumble into a decision or a reaction that ultimately proves very wrong.

And they end up destroying the fruit of the Spirit in their lives.

It's not our deliberate disobedience that causes most of our problems—it's our ignorant folly. It's not our love of evil that defeats us, but our *ignorance* of the deceitful schemes of Satan. We want to do good, but the flesh fools us into trying to do good *our* way instead of *God's* way.

And that is how the Haman within each of us deceives and deludes the king within each of us.

In Esther 4, we began to see God's reaction to such folly. We see how God sets about to save us from our own mad choices. As we pick up the story, we see Mordecai's first reaction to Haman's plot. It is a manifestation of what we might call good and godly grief:

> When Mordecai learned of all that had been done, he tore his clothes, put on sackcloth and ashes, and went out into the city, wailing loudly and bitterly. But he went only as far as the king's gate, because no one clothed in sackcloth was allowed to enter it. In every province to which the edict and order of the king came, there was great mourning among the Jews, with fasting, weeping and wailing. Many lay in sackcloth and ashes (Esther 4:1–3).

What a picture of grief! Lay this passage alongside these words from the New Testament: "And do not grieve the Holy Spirit of God, with whom you were sealed for the day of redemption" (Ephesians 4:30). As we have previously seen, Mordecai can be seen to symbolize the Holy Spirit within us. His grief, then, is a symbol of the grief God's own Spirit feels when we stumble into folly, sin, and error.

How does God react to the folly of human choice when we follow the promptings of the flesh? He grieves! He wears sackcloth and ashes, as it were, and He mourns over the sorrow and pain we have brought upon ourselves. And what is it that grieves the Holy Spirit? What are the human actions that grieve Him? Paul gives us the answer in the next verse: "Get rid of all bitterness, rage and anger, brawling and slander, along with every form of malice" (Ephesians 4:31).

These are the actions that grieve the Spirit. Notice that these actions are the opposite of those attitudes Paul calls "the fruit of the Spirit"— love, joy, peace, patience, kindness, goodness, faithfulness, gentleness, and self-control. This is why the apostle Paul adds, "Be kind and compassionate to one another, forgiving each other, just as in Christ God forgave you" (Ephesians 4:32).

So the theme of Esther 4 is grief—the grief of Mordecai, which mirrors and symbolizes the grief that we, as Christians, inflict on the Holy Spirit through our folly and sin.

GRIEF OVER CONSEQUENCES

When Mordecai learned of the choice the king had made—a choice to eradicate the people of God—he was moved with sorrow. He cried out loudly and bitterly—a poignant picture of the grief of the Holy Spirit. It's remarkable to see that what grieves the heart of God is not so much the enmity of the sinner as it is the foolishness of the saint!

Let's take a closer look at the grief of Mordecai and apply the lessons of this story to our own lives.

Mordecai knew that the edict of King Xerxes was bound up in the unchangeable law of the Medes and Persians. Once the king's decision was announced, the consequences of that decision were inevitable. Even the king could not change it once it had been signed and sealed.

Why did Mordecai mourn so? We know that he had faith that God would deliver the Jewish people in spite of the king's edict. How do we know this? Because in verse 14, Mordecai expresses confidence that "relief and deliverance for the Jews will arise from another place." Although the name of God is never explicitly mentioned, it is clear that Mordecai placed his trust in God to deliver the Jews. He was confident that deliverance would come by one means or another.

Yet he mourned because he knew that some suffering was inevitable because of the king's decision. In the same way, the Holy Spirit knows that the will of God cannot be thwarted by human choices and events. Nevertheless, the Spirit grieves over our sin and folly because sin always produces suffering. Some of the consequences of sin and folly cannot be avoided or reversed. That is why the Spirit grieves.

I once had a conversation with a young man of about thirty. Despite his youth, his hair was white and he looked much older than his true age. When I remarked about his white hair, he smiled rather ruefully and said, "The Lord saved me from my sin, but the marks of sin are still there." Even though our sins are forgiven, the Spirit grieves over the marks of sin that remain.

There's a story of a father whose son repeatedly caused trouble and chaos in the family. After each painful incident, he would come to his father, say, "I'm sorry, Dad," and his father would forgive him. But the boy seemed cavalier about his sins. He acted as if he felt entitled to forgiveness, as if all one has to do is say, "I'm sorry," and the incident is over as if it never happened. The young man seemed to have no awareness of the suffering his sin and rebellion caused his mother and father.

So the father said to the son, "Let's go out to the garage. I want to show you something." In the garage, the father took a hammer and nail, and he pounded the nail into the garage wall. Then he handed the hammer to his son and said, "Now, son, I want you to pull out the nail."

The son shrugged, used the claw end of the hammer, and pulled out the nail.

The father said, "That's like forgiveness, isn't it? When you do something wrong, it's like pounding in a nail. Forgiveness is when you pull the nail out again."

"Yeah," the son said. "I can see that."

"Fine," said the father. "Now, I want you to take that hammer and pull out the nail hole."

The startled young man said, "But I can't make the hole go away!" And then his father's meaning became clear. Forgiveness can erase the offense, but it cannot erase the consequences. Sin and folly always produce consequences that do not go away, even by forgiveness.

The law of the Medes and Persians could never be changed, and that is why Mordecai wept. In the same way, the law of consequences cannot be changed—and that is why the Holy Spirit grieves over our sin.

"JESUS WEPT"

Mordecai wept not only for his own people but perhaps also for the king and the kingdom because of the sorrow they had unwittingly brought upon themselves. Mordecai knew that the Jews were under special protection from God wherever they were. As a Jew, he was aware that no nation could lay a hand upon the Jews without suffering the consequences. This has been true throughout history.

The Egyptians enslaved the Jews. The Amalekites attacked the Jews. The Babylonians carried the Jews into exile. The Romans conquered and oppressed the Jews. The Nazis under Adolf Hitler tried to exterminate the Jews. The Arab nations of the Middle East have repeatedly tried to wipe the Jewish nation off the map.

But down through the centuries, God has kept the promise He made to Abraham: "I will make you into a great nation and I will bless you; I will make your name great, and you will be a blessing. I will bless those who bless you, and whoever curses you I will curse; and all peoples on earth will be blessed through you" (Genesis 12:2–3).

Mordecai knew that if the king of Persia carried out this plot against God's people, the Persian Empire itself would be defeated, just as every nation has been defeated that ever raised its fist in anger against God's chosen people. So he grieved—not only for his own people but also for the people of Persia, who would suffer as a result of the folly of their king.

And remember that we are looking at this true story as a parable of our own lives. The Spirit knows that when we unthinkingly allow ourselves to be controlled by our sin nature, we defeat ourselves in the process. The sin nature, the flesh, creates tensions, pressures, addictions, behaviors, and compulsions that tear us apart and set us at odds with ourselves and the people around us. So the Spirit weeps out of sympathy for those who afflict themselves and others by their sin and folly.

We see this spirit of grief in our Lord Jesus as he went to the tomb of his friend Lazarus. John 11:35 tells us that as He approached the tomb, "Jesus wept." In the original Greek, the language conveys that He "burst into tears" with an overflow of emotion. Jesus knew that within moments he would speak the words that would call Lazarus forth from the tomb. All grief would be miraculously turned to joy—yet at that moment, Jesus wept. Why?

He wept because he knew, as few of us know, the true meaning of death, which is the result of sin. He grieved over the death of Lazarus because His friend had suffered death as a consequence of sin. His grieving over Lazarus was like the grieving of the Spirit over you and me. The Spirit knows that we will ultimately be saved from our sin and folly, but He also knows that we cannot escape the consequences of sin.

Thank God for the grief of the Spirit. His grieving proves the unwillingness of God to let us go on stumbling into the bottomless pit of our own folly.

QUENCHING THE SPIRIT

Mordecai has gone out to the city, dressed in sackcloth and ashes, mourning loudly and bitterly—yet neither King Xerxes nor Queen Esther is aware of Mordecai's grief. So it is with you and me. We sin, we behave foolishly, and we grieve the Holy Spirit—yet we are usually unaware of how the Spirit mourns over us.

The next few verses reveal the results in the human spirit once the grieving of the Holy Spirit is made known. It's a picture of intense spiritual distress. The first step is an uneasy realization that something is deeply wrong. We read:

> When Esther's maids and eunuchs came and told her about Mordecai, she was in great distress. She sent clothes for him to put on instead of his sackcloth, but he would not accept them (Esther 4:4).

Esther's actions are fascinating and instructive. When she learns that Mordecai is in deep grief and distress, wearing sackcloth and ashes, she responds by sending him a change of clothes. Even though she surely understands the meaning of sackcloth as a symbol of mourning, she seems to think that new clothes will put Mordecai in a better mood. She doesn't understand the problem, so she offers a woefully inadequate solution.

Many of us, when confronted by someone who is grieving or in distress, try to correct the problem with a superficial solution. It's as if we have encountered someone with a gunshot wound, and we offer a Band-Aid. Instead of offering hasty and inappropriate "solutions" that solve nothing, we would do well to listen to people in their distress and find out where they really hurt and what they really need.

Eventually, Mordecai was able to make Esther understand the grave threat faced by the Jewish people. When she understood the nature of Mordecai's grief, she was able to make an appropriate response.

The grief of Mordecai symbolizes the grief of the Holy Spirit. Have you ever become aware, somewhere in the depths of your spirit, that you have grieved the Spirit of God? You don't know specifically what you have done, but deep within, you know something is wrong with your relationship with God. That's the realization we see pictured here in parable form.

Because Mordecai symbolically represents the Holy Spirit, it's important to understand what it means when we see Queen Esther trying to placate Mordecai's grief with a gift of clothing. Her first response to Mordecai's grief was to try to silence his wailing and cover up his sackcloth with new clothes. In other words, she tried to *quench* Mordecai's grief instead of asking him *why* he was grieving.

In 1 Thessalonians 5, Paul writes, "Do not put out the Spirit's fire" (v. 19), or, in the King James Version, "Quench not the Spirit." In other words, when we sense the Holy Spirit speaking to us and trying to bring a matter to our attention, we should not try to silence His voice. Instead, we should listen to what the Spirit is saying to us—and we should act upon what He tells us.

At this point, a word of caution is in order. We need to distinguish carefully between the condemning voice of Satan and the true grief that comes from the Holy Spirit. Satan will sometimes afflict us with a vague sense of guilt designed to trap us into legalism, which is the effort of the flesh to placate guilt through religious activity or good works. You probably know that vague, nagging sense of guilt and condemnation. Satan knows that if he can get us focused on feelings so that we begin to operate in the flesh instead of the Spirit, he can blunt our effectiveness for God.

By contrast, the voice of the Spirit is always specific and to the point. The Spirit is never vague. If He is speaking to you, then you know what He wants you to do. You may try to avoid it, you may shove it from your mind, but you cannot escape the prompting of the Spirit. He is insistent because His love for you is relentless. The voice of the grieved Spirit within will lead to a clear revelation of sin.

We see that revelation in parable form in the next few verses:

> Then Esther summoned Hathach, one of the king's eunuchs assigned to attend her, and ordered him to find out what was troubling Mordecai and why.
>
> So Hathach went out to Mordecai in the open square of the city in front of the king's gate. Mordecai told him everything that had happened to him, including the exact amount of money Haman had promised to pay into the royal treasury for the destruction of the Jews. He also gave him a copy of the text of the edict for their annihilation, which had been published in Susa, to show to Esther and explain it to her, and he told him to urge her to go into the king's presence to beg for mercy and plead with him for her people.
>
> Hathach went back and reported to Esther what Mordecai had said (Esther 4:5–9).

Notice how clear and specific this revelation is. Mordecai knew the whole story. He knew the exact sum of money that Haman, in secret, had told the king he would put into his treasury, and he had a copy of the decree. He revealed the whole plan in exacting detail. The text does not tell us how Mordecai came in possession of this information, but he probably had one or more informants in the palace—perhaps one of the king's own servants.

It's significant that the name of the servant who acted as an intermediary is *Hathach,* which means "truth." When you know that some obscuring cloud of sin has come between you and the Lord, where do you go for insight and understanding? To the Word of Truth, of course! Often, while we read the Scriptures in our daily devotions, we find that the Spirit of God illuminates a particular passage so that it speaks directly and specifically to us.

We must read the Word of Truth—and we must listen to the Spirit of Truth. Often, while in prayer and communion with God, we realize that something is wrong in our lives. So we'll ask God to make it clear, and suddenly an image will come to mind of a person we have offended or a sin that is unrepented. The Spirit of Truth brings that image to mind. Through His Word and His Spirit, God makes His truth known to us, just as He set the truth of this matter before Queen Esther.

THE RELUCTANCE OF THE QUEEN

Next, we see—to our amazement—reluctance on the part of Queen Esther:

> Then she instructed him to say to Mordecai, "All the king's officials and the people of the royal provinces know that for any man or woman who approaches the king in the inner court without being summoned the king has but one law: that he be put to death. The only exception to this is for the king to extend the gold scepter to him and spare his life. But thirty days have passed since I was called to go to the king" (Esther 4:10–11).

Once again, we catch a profound glimpse of the inner workings of our own hearts. Remember, the king represents the soul—the mind, emotions, and will. There is a definite danger in confronting the soul unexpectedly because the soul is such a creature of moods. If the queen (representing the spirit) approaches the king (representing the soul) while he is in an unreceptive mood, it might upset the whole kingdom!

God, through the Holy Spirit, plans His approach in such a way as to catch us in the right mood. In our conscious mind we are often reluctant to consider unpleasant truths. This may explain why our dreams sometimes present symbols of fears, insecurities, guilt, and other unpleasant realities that our waking, conscious mind refuses to ponder.

Esther is reluctant to approach the king too soon and too abruptly. He needs to be handled with care because he is subject to his own reasoning and emotions, and he is a creature of changing moods.

Upon receiving Esther's message, Mordecai responds insistently. We read:

> When Esther's words were reported to Mordecai, he sent back this answer: "Do not think that because you are in the king's house you alone of all the Jews will escape. For if you remain silent at this time, relief and deliverance for the Jews will arise from another place, but you and your father's family will perish. And who knows but that you have come to royal position for such a time as this?"
>
> Then Esther sent this reply to Mordecai: "Go, gather together all the Jews who are in Susa, and fast for me. Do not eat or drink for three days, night or day. I and my maids will fast as you do. When this is done, I will go to the king, even though it is against the law. And if I perish, I perish."
>
> So Mordecai went away and carried out all of Esther's instructions (Esther 4:12–17).

Mordecai replies to the reluctant Queen Esther that the fact that she is queen does not ensure her safety. If the king's edict is carried out, all of the Jews will be slaughtered—including Esther herself. Moreover, if she remains silent, God will still see to it that the Jews are delivered—but by a different means. Esther will not have the honor of being used by God.

Next, we read the most memorable lines of the book of Esther. Mordecai concludes with these profound words, which speak not only to the conscience of the queen but also to your heart and mine: "And who knows but that you have come to royal position for such a time as this?"

God has an infinite number of ways to accomplish His will. When God makes His will known to us, you and I may still fail to carry it out. That is our choice. But our failure cannot prevent God's plan from being accomplished. If you or I fail Him, He will raise up another, or accomplish His purpose in some other way. God is never hindered by human failure.

But when we fail Him, we miss out on the beauty of God's perfect will for our lives. We "suffer loss," as Paul puts it in 1 Corinthians 3:15.

THE COURAGE OF THE QUEEN

Mordecai's reply awakens a sense of spiritual distress within Queen Esther. She replies with a willingness to act—and even a willingness to die. She sends word back to Mordecai, asking him to gather the Jews in the city for three days of fasting. Then, she says, "I will go to the king, even though it is against the law. And if I perish, I perish."

As we have previously seen, the story of Esther becoming the queen of Persia is a picture in parable form of Christian conversion. What is the purpose of conversion? What did God have in mind for you when He saved you? Was it only that He might take you to heaven some day? Is it that you might have glory in the sweet by-and-by? No! He saved you so that you could know Him and join Him in His great plan for human history. Like Queen Esther herself, God has brought you into His kingdom, into this royal position you now hold, *for such a time as this*!

When God saved you by grace through faith in Jesus Christ, His desire was that you might live a life of fruitfulness and victory. He saved you so that right now, right here where you live and work, you might manifest the fullness of the character of God. Your conversion was merely the beginning of a great adventure with God. He planned to give you victory over bitterness, resentment, malice, anger, lust, and every other manifestation of the flesh. If you are learning and growing and experiencing that victory, then you are living out God's plan and purpose for your life. He has truly brought you into His kingdom for such a time as this.

When Esther tells Mordecai to gather all the Jews in the city of Susa to fast on her behalf, she is prophetically prefiguring the death of Christ. Notice that she calls for the Jews to fast for three days. This is no coincidence. Esther may not have known it, but she was calling upon the Jews to symbolize an event that is yet to come: The death and resurrection of Jesus Christ. For three days He lay in the grave, where He could not eat and could not drink. This identified Esther with the death of Christ and with the three days He spent in the tomb.

Then, at the end of those three days, she arose to go before the king. If you were to lay Paul's letter to the Romans alongside the book of Esther, you would find that we now stand before this passage:

> What shall we say, then? Shall we go on sinning so that grace may increase? By no means! We died to sin; how can we live in it any longer? Or don't you know that all of us who were baptized into Christ Jesus were baptized into his death? We were therefore buried with him through baptism into death in order that, just as Christ was raised from the dead through the glory of the Father, we too may live a new life (Romans 6:1 4).

This is the place where daily deliverance begins. How beautifully Esther's words picture for us this identification of the believer with the death of Jesus Christ. All deliverance from death and sin stems from this fundamental declaration: We are identified with Christ and with His death. We may not always feel like Christians. At times, we may not even act like Christians. But if we are identified with Christ and with His death, we are dead to sin and alive in Christ.

We desperately need to lay hold of this truth. Until we begin to truly believe that we are crucified with Christ, buried with Him, and raised with Him, we will never have the confidence to accept the deliverance He has given us. Once you know you are crucified with Christ, your life will never be the same again. Your deliverance from sin and death rests upon this unchangeable truth.

I once had a conversation with a young man who had stopped attending our church for a while. I asked him why he no longer came on Sunday mornings.

"Well," he said, "I hesitate to come anymore because I feel like a hypocrite. When I'm at work, I can't seem to live like a Christian ought to. I lose my temper, I swear, I treat my co-workers badly—and then, if I come to church, I feel like I'm living a lie."

I said, "You know, a hypocrite is someone who acts like something he isn't. When you come to church, are you acting like a Christian or a non-Christian?"

"Well," he said, "I'd be acting like a Christian if I came to church. But after the way I've been living in the world, I'd be a hypocrite, wouldn't I?"

I said, "Are you a Christian?"

"Yes, I am."

"All right, then. If you are a Christian, then when is it that you do not act like one? In church or at work?"

"Oh!" he said. "I see what you mean. I'm being a hypocrite at work!"

"Exactly," I said. "When you come to church, you're being what you really are for perhaps the first time during that week. So what you need to do is to stop being a hypocrite at work."

With that new perspective on his life, he went back into the world—asking God for the strength to live like a Christian seven days a week.

It's not hypocritical to come among the people of God when you know you've failed. You belong in the church whether you feel strong or weak, whether you are successful or a miserable failure. That's what Christians are—people who are saved by grace, people who love the Lord, people who sometimes fail and need a fresh touch of His grace all over again.

Like my young friend, you may sometimes be a hypocrite during the week—at home, at work, at the market, or driving around in your car. If you wish to stop being a hypocrite, don't give up God's people. Give up your worldliness. Apply your faith to your everyday life every day of the week.

The key to living like a Christian is to live in the knowledge that we are identified with Christ. We have died with Him, and we are raised with Him. When that is your perspective on life, you cease to see yourself as a worldling who puts on a Sunday act. You begin to see yourself as a Christian who occasionally stumbles and acts like a worldling. When you fail, the Spirit of God is grieved—and He will bring it to your attention, so that you may repent, be forgiven, and be restored to sweet fellowship with Him.

Next, we shall explore Esther 5, which opens with these words: "On the third day Esther put on her royal robes and stood in the inner court of the palace, in front of the king's hall" (Esther 5:1). Mark those words: "On the third day," the day of resurrection, the day of new life—Queen Esther went in to see the king.

This is your clue to the theme of Esther 5!

6

SOUL AND SPIRIT

Esther 5

*A*s I said at the beginning of this book, the story of Esther reads like a novel—and we have now come to one of the most dramatic moments in this fast-paced, intricately woven plot.

The king of ancient Persia has married a beautiful Jewish girl named Esther, who was raised by her cousin, Mordecai. But the prime minister of the kingdom is a loathsome villain named Haman, who has hatched a plot to take revenge against Mordecai by killing all the Jews in Persia. The king—seduced by Haman's manipulative scheme and completely unaware that his own queen is a Jew—issues a proclamation calling for genocide against the Jewish people. When Mordecai learns of the plot, he urges Queen Esther to risk the king's disfavor by going to him uninvited to plead for the lives of her people.

But the story of Esther is much more than a fascinating tale that reads like a suspenseful novel. And it is even more than an account of historical events that took place in the ancient world. The story of Esther can also be seen as a divinely inspired portrayal of the spiritual principles that govern your life and mine in these times in which we live.

You are a living soul, the king over a kingdom that is the empire of your life. If you are a Christian, your spirit was made alive in Jesus Christ. Your regenerated spirit is the queen that has come into your life. Mordecai, in this story, is a figure of the Holy Spirit moving to preserve the fruit of the Spirit in the kingdom of your life. And the people of Mordecai, the Jews, represent the fruit of the Spirit.

And the villain of the story? Haman represents what the Bible calls "the flesh" or "the sinful nature," the depraved ego, the fallen self. The Haman-like flesh is slyly at work in our minds. It is cunning and subtle, whispering to us that the key to "the good life" lies in choosing our own way instead of God's way. That's the aim of the flesh in the life of the believer.

Satan knows that if he can seduce a Christian into operating in the flesh instead of in the Spirit, then that Christian's ministry will be rendered null and void as far as God is concerned. This is the great battlefield of the Christian life. This battle is raging in your life at this very moment. And this is the battle that is depicted in parable form in the book of Esther.

THE SOUL AND THE SPIRIT

Last chapter, when we left Esther, she was standing outside the king's hall, wondering if she would be received by the king—or executed for her presumptuousness. Her final message to Mordecai: "If I perish, I perish."

It has been said that courage is not the absence of fear; it is the willingness to do the very thing we fear most. According to this definition, Queen Esther is a trembling mass of courage! Her heart is in her mouth. She knows that King Xerxes is subject to moods and whims. There's no way to predict how he will respond when she walks into the king's hall. We pick up the story in Esther 5:

> On the third day Esther put on her royal robes and stood in the inner court of the palace, in front of the king's hall. The king was sitting on his royal throne in the hall, facing the entrance. When he saw Queen Esther standing in the court, he was pleased with her and held out to her the gold scepter that was in his hand. So Esther approached and touched the tip of the scepter.
>
> Then the king asked, "What is it, Queen Esther? What is your request? Even up to half the kingdom, it will be given you" (Esther 5:1–3).

Queen Esther's courage is rewarded! The king is in a good mood, and he is delighted to see her. With his golden scepter, he invites her to approach and offers to grant any request, even up to half his kingdom. (If Esther had actually asked for half the kingdom, the king's mood might have soured considerably!)

Let's pause for a moment and consider what this true story—which we are examining as a parable for teaching purposes—means for your life and mine. It's interesting to note the distinction between the human soul and the human spirit, as pictured for us by the distinction between the king and his queen. Most of us are completely unaware of any difference at all between our own soul and spirit. We tend to look at ourselves as an undivided single unit: spirit, soul, mind, emotions, will, head, body, limbs, fingers, toes—we think of all of this as "me."

Scientists have built microscopes that can photograph the atom and telescopes that can detect planets circling distant stars. They have mapped the human genome and unlocked the secrets of the human cell. But the greatest mystery of all remains unsolved—the mystery of our own nature. We do not understand ourselves. We have a sense that we are more than a temporary assemblage of cells and tissues, fluids and organs, which lives and dies and is no more. We sense that there is an "I" that exists, distinct from the body, which will go on even after the body dies. But what is that mysterious "I"?

I recall how my little daughter, then three years old, climbed up on my chest as I lay in bed one morning. She tried to wake me, but I teased her, pretending to be asleep. She pinched me and poked me, but I refused to open my eyes. Finally, she reached her hand to my face, pried open one of my eyes, and said, "Are you in there, Daddy?"

That was a startling insight. I realized at that moment that even a toddler is aware that there is more to a human being than a body. A person is somehow "in there," inside the body.

What is harder for us to understand is that the person who is "in there"—this inner being we innately *know* to be dwelling within our bodies—is actually divided into two parts that the Bible calls "spirit" and "soul." Paul makes this distinction in 1 Thessalonians 5:23: "May your whole spirit, soul and body be kept blameless at the coming of our Lord Jesus Christ." And we find the same distinction again in Hebrews 4:12,

69

which says that the Word of God "penetrates even to dividing soul and spirit."

Psychology tells us that the human personality is divided into both conscious and subconscious components. The conscious component consists of that which the Bible calls the soul. It is the conscious part of ourselves that contains the mind (our ability to think, remember, and reason), the emotions (our ability to feel and empathize), and the will (our power to choose and act). The mind and emotions continually interact with each other, and together they affect the will. The soul is the king that reigns over the kingdom of our lives.

And what of the subconscious component of the human personality? This is certainly a deeper and hidden part of ourselves that is sometimes referred to as the subconscious. Is the subconscious component the same thing the Bible calls "the spirit"? Perhaps, though we can't be certain. The subconscious area of life is, for many people, a dark and confused aspect of the self. Its impulses and motives are often mysterious, shaped by hurts and traumas of the past, but whether the subconscious self corresponds to the spirit is something we can't say for certain.

Like the soul, the human spirit is fallible and fallen. The conscience is a function of the spirit, yet the conscience can be wrong. I once heard of a cannibal who suffered from a guilty conscience because he had not killed as many enemies as his father had. Clearly, his conscience was terribly misguided.

But whether or not we can accurately say that the subconscious self is the same as the spirit, I believe it is possible for you and me to detect the existence of a distinct spirit within us, separate from the soul.

You have probably had an experience where someone did or said something to you that caused you to suddenly lose your temper. Even as you began to respond, you sensed a voice inside you saying, "Don't blow up! You'll only embarrass yourself! You'll ruin this relationship! You'll look like a fool if you don't get yourself under control!" But you ignored this voice, you exploded in anger, and you let loose a blistering tirade.

Later, just as that little inner voice predicted, you were sorry, you were embarrassed, and you apologized, saying, "I don't know what came over me. It was as if I was standing outside myself, watching myself lose control and say all those awful things." People sometimes describe that feeling as being "beside myself with anger," because they literally feel as if they are two distinct selves—one who behaves angrily and irrationally, and the other who watches this display in horror and disbelief.

I believe that when our soulish emotions fly out of control, our spirit stands back and pleads with the soul, warns the soul—and grieves when the soul refuses to listen. The next time you feel "beside yourself," remember this illustration of the soul and the spirit. It is this division of soul and spirit that is visibly represented for us by the king as he is cautiously approached by Queen Esther.

CAPTIVATED BY BEAUTY

Into this darkened life of ours came the light of Jesus Christ. We received Him as our Lord, and He began to assert His authority and lordship over our lives. We were born again. The spirit within us was made alive by the quickening power of Jesus Christ. Our spirit became a place of glory and beauty under the control of the Holy Spirit, who dwells within. The glory and light of God filled us, and the guidance we received from our human spirit, indwelt by the Holy Spirit, was true, realistic, and clear.

Once we have been made alive in resurrection power by the life of Jesus Christ, our human spirit becomes the means through which the Holy Spirit seeks to influence and repossess the soul—the mind, emotions, and will. This is why it is difficult in certain Scripture passages to distinguish between the human spirit and the Holy Spirit. Translators frequently have a problem determining whether to spell *spirit* with a lower case *s* or a capital *S*. The renewed human spirit is fully subject to the control of the Holy Spirit, so that the two are working together constantly.

The human soul, however, is a different matter altogether. The soul is the king of the kingdom of your life. Being a king, the soul has the power to reject the pleadings of the Spirit if it so chooses. This truth is what we see portrayed for us in the book of Esther.

Queen Esther is reluctant to come before the king because he has the power to deny her if he pleases. In the same way, in our own lives, the will of the soul is supreme. Every action in our lives is subject to the judgment of the soul—and the soul has the power to reject the pleadings of the spirit.

When Esther comes before the king, he is captivated by her beauty, and he is instantly prepared to grant her desire. For three days and nights, she has been fasting as though dead. Now, on the third day, she appears before the king, a beautiful picture of the resurrection life of our Lord Jesus. She symbolically represents the fact that the Spirit of God always approaches us on the basis of the risen life of Christ.

The way Queen Esther approaches the king is the same way the Spirit approaches us when He wants us to surrender our will on a particular matter. The Spirit doesn't condemn us. He doesn't punish us. He doesn't thunder at us. Rather, He comes to us in all His grace and beauty. Then, when our hearts have been melted by His grace, we are ready to say, "Whatever I have is Yours, Lord. I'll do whatever You say."

A friend told me about something he saw while driving down the highway. Ahead of him was a large truck, a moving van. On the rear of the truck was a sign that read, "Any Load, Any Time, Any Distance, Any Place."

"That sign spoke to me," he said. "That is exactly what my heart says when I see the beauty of Jesus Christ. That is the response of my heart when I am grateful for His presence in my life: 'Lord Jesus, any load, any distance, any time, any place.'"

That should be the response of your heart and mine to the urgings and entreaties of the Holy Spirit in us.

WHY THE DELAY?

Esther comes before the king in her beauty and glory, and the king is instantly ready to grant her desire. Strangely, Esther declines to state her desire. Instead, we read:

> "If it pleases the king," replied Esther, "let the king, together with Haman, come today to a banquet I have prepared for him."

"Bring Haman at once," the king said, "so that we may do what Esther asks."

So the king and Haman went to the banquet Esther had prepared. As they were drinking wine, the king again asked Esther, "Now what is your petition? It will be given you. And what is your request? Even up to half the kingdom, it will be granted."

Esther replied, "My petition and my request is this: If the king regards me with favor and if it pleases the king to grant my petition and fulfill my request, let the king and Haman come tomorrow to the banquet I will prepare for them. Then I will answer the king's question" (Esther 5:4–8).

Why does Esther put the king off? Why doesn't she simply reveal her request? She has him right where she wants him. There seems to be no good reason for delay. He's in a good mood, eager to grant her anything she wants. He is like putty in her hands, eager to give her anything she asks. Why, then, does she delay?

Have you ever had a similar experience in your relationship with the Lord? Have you ever come to the place where, captivated by the beauty of Christ and sensing the glory and joy He brings, you have dedicated yourself to Him and offered yourself to Him? Perhaps you have gone forward in a meeting or you've raised your hand or you've knelt in the secrecy of your own room and committed yourself anew to Christ. Then you waited for God to act.

And nothing happened.

You thought that God might lead you into some new ministry or even send you out to the mission field. But the doors didn't open. The call didn't come. And you asked yourself, "Why does God delay? I'm yielded, I'm ready, Lord, send me!" But nothing happens. How do you explain it?

The story of Queen Esther suggests two reasons:

First, God is never content with a decision that is based on emotions alone. We have already seen that Haman can persuade the king as easily as Esther can. If his decisions are based on emotions alone, those decisions will continuously shift back and forth with every changing wind. This is why so many Christians seem spiritually unstable—their spiritual experience is rooted in their emotions and feelings, not in the steady and dependable counsel of God's Spirit and God's Word.

Emotions are an aspect of the soul, not the spirit. Although God is interested in every aspect of our lives, including our emotions, He does not want us to respond to Him solely in our emotions. He desires our true spirituality, not merely our emotionalism. So when the moment of our surrender takes place, God frequently delays action in order to give us time to think the matter through. He is giving us time to allow our spiritual understanding to catch up with our emotions.

When I was a young, growing Christian, I wanted to be a surgeon. Even as a little boy in elementary school, I would sit at my desk and manipulate my fingers so my knuckles would be supple enough to tie delicate surgical knots. I haunted every hospital I could get to. I read every book on the medical arts that I could find. I studied the parts of the body—the nerves and muscles, the organs and bones—while still in high school.

Then, very quietly, something changed within me. I don't know how or when or why it happened. I only know that I began to realize that God was moving in a different direction, and He was suggesting to me that I consider entering the ministry.

At first I resented His leading away from medicine and toward the pulpit. I fought against it, resisting the plea of the Spirit. But when the Spirit is after someone, He never gives up. Finally, in a moment of surrender and dedication, alone in my own room, I said to him, "All right, Lord, I'll be a minister if that is what you want."

But then nothing happened!

I expected an invitation the next day to preach at some prominent church, but it didn't come. I waited, and I continued doing the things that were before me to do.

When I left the city of Chicago, I went to Denver; and from there, after a year or so, I went out to Honolulu. By this time, World War II had begun. I began teaching Bible classes in bomb shelters, but still no doors were opening that led toward the ministry. It wasn't until the war ended and I was discharged from the service that the Lord cleared a path for me to enter seminary.

Once I arrived at Dallas Theological Seminary, I discovered that I was much better prepared for ministry training than I would have been several years earlier. Having spent some time traveling, living in the world, and teaching small-group Bible studies, I had a much better grasp of what was involved in full-time ministry. I was able to learn much more in seminary because I knew what the spiritual battlefield of the ministry was like.

God knows that the king within each of us needs time—time to make wise, Spirit-led decisions that are based on more than mere emotional impulses. Emotions often prompt faith, but if our understanding doesn't catch up to our emotions, the faith can die as soon as the emotions fade.

That's why Jesus said, "If you hold to my teaching, you are really my disciples" (John 8:31). Many people came to Jesus and followed Him on the basis of emotions. They were excited by His miracles, they were moved by His compassion, they were stirred by His preaching—but emotion is not enough to sustain genuine faith. Only those who truly hold to the Lord's teaching are *really* His disciples. If you hold to His teachings, Jesus said, "you will know the truth, and the truth will set you free" (v. 32).

HAMAN'S DELUSION

The second reason God sometimes delays becomes apparent in the final verses of this passage—a section we might call "Haman's Delusion." We read:

> Haman went out that day happy and in high spirits. But when he saw Mordecai at the king's gate and observed that he neither rose nor showed fear in his presence, he was filled with rage against Mordecai. Nevertheless, Haman restrained himself and went home.
>
> Calling together his friends and Zeresh, his wife, Haman boasted to them about his vast wealth, his many sons, and all the ways the king had honored him and how he had elevated him above the other nobles and officials. "And that's not all," Haman added. "I'm the only person Queen Esther invited to accompany the king to the banquet she gave. And she has invited me along with the king tomorrow. But

all this gives me no satisfaction as long as I see that Jew Mordecai sitting at the king's gate."

His wife Zeresh and all his friends said to him, "Have a gallows built, seventy-five feet high, and ask the king in the morning to have Mordecai hanged on it. Then go with the king to the dinner and be happy." This suggestion delighted Haman, and he had the gallows built (Esther 5:9–14).

God's delay, as we see here, gives opportunity for the flesh (symbolized by Haman) to swell up with a sense of its own importance. In his arrogance, Haman drops all semblance of subtlety and brazenly displays the corruption of the flesh. Proverbs says, "Pride goes before destruction, a haughty spirit before a fall" (16:18).

The Holy Spirit allows our simple hearts to display what we think is hidden within. When our evil and corruption bursts forth, the sight is shocking and disgusting. The works of the flesh are truly loathsome. As Jesus said, "There is nothing concealed that will not be disclosed, or hidden that will not be made known" (Luke 12:2).

Haman thinks he has won *both* the king and the queen to his side. He is jubilant! But his cheerful mood is short-lived. Reaching the king's gate, he encounters Mordecai, who once again refuses to bow before him. Though enraged, Haman manages to restrain himself and goes home. There he gathers his wife and friends, and he brags to them about his riches, his sons, his favored position with the king, and his status, which now dwarfs that of all the other Persian noblemen and officials.

Nothing feeds the narcissistic ego like an audience of attentive admirers. Nothing soothes our wounded pride like having others sit in rapt attention as we brag about our own prowess. To this ancient Persian, the symbols of status were riches and sons and the honor of the king.

To today's American males, the symbols of status might be a big house, a country-club membership, and a car that goes from zero to sixty in 3.95 seconds. Why? Because the big house conveys wealth, the country club suggests acceptance and popularity, and the fast car symbolizes power—a high-octane, gas-guzzling extension of one's manhood. Men easily mistake the virtues of a machine for their own virtues. What a profound revelation of the Haman-like human heart!

The example of Haman reveals one of the basic weaknesses of the flesh, of human evil. This is why Christians have nothing to fear from the presence of evil in the world. Jesus told us that when the world seems to be crashing down all around us, when human hearts are failing for fear, then "stand up and lift up your heads, because your redemption is drawing near" (see Luke 21:28). This is why we can be assured that no form of totalitarianism will ever conquer the earth. Nazism has already failed. Atheistic communism is doomed to fail. Islamic terrorism is likewise doomed. The seeds of self-destruction are built into every form of evil that seeks to dominate our world. As the hymnist Maltbie Davenport Babcock (1858-1901) wrote:

> This is my Father's world. O let me ne'er forget
> That though the wrong seems oft so strong, God is the ruler yet.
> This is my Father's world: the battle is not done:
> Jesus Who died shall be satisfied,
> And earth and Heav'n be one.

Murderous, self-centered pride comes from our human nature, the Haman nature within us. And pride produces delusion. Pride blinds us to the truth about ourselves and the world around us. When human beings are blinded by pride, they easily stumble into folly. When you and I give way to pride, we allow Haman to rule our lives. We become willfully stupid. We make decisions to our own detriment. And then, when we incur the consequences of our own prideful, foolish decisions, we try to cast the blame on others, on God, on anything or anyone but ourselves.

I once heard of a nurse who was working in a hospital. While going on her rounds, she encountered a patient who said something that angered her. She lost her temper and exploded in rage, heaping abuse upon her patient.

Just then, the nurse's supervisor happened to pass in the hall. Hearing the nurse's tirade, the supervisor called the nurse out in the hall and reprimanded her for her unprofessional behavior. The nurse was instantly ashamed and stammered out an apology. "I don't know what came over me," she said.

"I don't know either," the supervisor replied. "I didn't know you were that kind of person."

"Oh, but I'm not!" the nurse replied. "That really wasn't me! It's just that I've been under pressure, and that patient said something that just set me off. But I'm really not like this!"

The supervisor said, "If you had a glass of water in your hand and I bumped your arm, what would slop out of the glass?"

"Water."

"Exactly. When you get 'bumped' by a disagreeable patient or a flat tire on your car or some other frustration, then whatever comes out of your mouth is what was already in you to begin with."

And the nurse had to acknowledge that the supervisor was right.

That's why Jesus said, "What goes into a man's mouth does not make him 'unclean,' but what comes out of his mouth, that is what makes him 'unclean'" (Matthew 15:11). The flesh is filled with evil and moral pollution, and as long as we refuse to admit the Haman-like corruption within us, we can never experience victory in our lives. The kindest thing God can do is to deflate our pride, even at the expense of our possessions and our reputation. Often it is only when we have been turned completely inside out that God can stand us right side up.

As we read the Gospels, we find that Jesus continually had to strip away the false pretenses from His disciples and show them exactly who and what they were. Several of them bickered over who would be the greatest in His kingdom. Peter bragged that even if all the other disciples forsook Jesus, he never would. Jesus had to peel away their pride and expose the corruption of the flesh before He could turn those failed and blundering disciples into true apostles.

The Lord Jesus also stripped away the false pretenses of the Pharisees. Those prideful, self-righteous Pharisees repeatedly tried to trap Him with theological questions. They worded their questions carefully, trying to anticipate every possible answer, hoping to discredit Him. In each instance, Jesus gave His opponents enough rope to hang themselves. Then

He answered their question in a totally unexpected way, leaving their hatred and deceitfulness exposed for all to see. The Pharisees hated Him for it—and that is why they plotted His death, the death of a criminal, death by crucifixion.

So it was with Haman. Mordecai's refusal to bow and scrape before Haman and his refusal to feed Haman's oversized ego filled the Persian prime minister with a murderous rage. As Haman considered what to do about Mordecai, his wife and friends said to him, "Have a gallows built, seventy-five feet high, and ask the king in the morning to have Mordecai hanged on it. Then go with the king to the dinner and be happy."

The text tells us that this suggestion "delighted" Haman, and he ordered that the instrument of Mordecai's execution be constructed forthwith.

As mentioned earlier, this word *gallows* can be misleading. In English, a gallows is a crossbeam stretched across two upright posts from which condemned prisoners are hanged at the end of a rope. In the original Hebrew, the word that is here translated *gallows* simply means "a timber or post." The victim would not be hanged from a rope; instead, he would be nailed to the post and impaled upon it, much as criminals in the Roman Empire would be nailed to crosses. (Incidentally, in the Sistine Chapel of the Vatican, Michelangelo painted a ceiling panel called *The Punishment of Haman* in which he accurately depicted Haman writhing in agony, nailed to a gnarled tree trunk.)

We must not lose sight of the significance of the exact manner of Haman's death. Haman was determined to crucify Mordecai. The flesh is always determined to crucify all that is good, all that is of God. This detail—Haman's determination to nail Mordecai to a wooden post, to torture and kill him by crucifixion—can be seen as a picture of the will of the flesh within each of us. There is something in us all that would willingly put Christ to death again if possible. You may resist that fact, you may deny it, but it is true.

Our most hopeful moment comes when we recognize that the flesh and all its corruption lurks within us, crying, "Crucify Him! Crucify Him!" It is there! Stop defending it! Treat the flesh, the sinful nature, as God directs you to.

Have you learned to recognize the Haman within you? Can you recognize him even when he comes smiling and dripping with oily charm? When someone slights you, insults you, cheats you, wastes your time, or hangs up on you, how do you feel? Do your teeth clench? Does your blood pressure rise? Do you want to get even? Do you want to teach that guy a lesson?

That's Haman! That's the flesh! That's exactly how Haman felt when Mordecai refused to bow to him in the king's gate. That is why Haman ordered a post to be erected so that his Jewish enemy could be impaled and tortured to death. The sin nature, the Haman within, put Jesus Christ on the cross 2,000 years ago—and it would do so again if it had the chance.

Haman—the sinful flesh—is our enemy.

But God, in His grace, drives us to our knees—not only in prayer, not only in humility, but also in recognition of the truth about ourselves. In His infinite love for us, He forces us to gaze into the mirror and see— *gasp!*—the face of Haman! He allows us to see what we are truly like without our pious Sunday morning mask. He permits us to see that lurking behind the mask is the leering flesh of Haman.

Praise God—He loves us too much to leave us in that state. Once we begin to see the flesh within us in honest terms, recognizing it for what it is, He makes a way for us to be healed of the corruption of the flesh. He has a plan for salvation. Our own plans can never work, but His will.

In Esther 6, God reveals that wonderful plan of deliverance to us!

7

THE PRICE OF SURVIVAL

Esther 6

One night in 1954, songwriter Irving Berlin lay awake in bed, unable to sleep. He had spent weeks writing the score for the Paramount Pictures motion picture *White Christmas*, but the film still lacked just the right song to make a certain scene sparkle. As Berlin tossed and turned well past midnight, his wife, Ellin, said to him, "Irving, you're keeping us *both* awake!"

"I can't help it," he said. "I've got insomnia again. I've tried everything—even counting sheep!"

"Well," she said, "why don't you try counting your blessings instead of sheep?"

He sat upright. "Hey!" he said. "I think you've got something there!"

"You're going to count your blessings?" Ellin asked.

"No, I'm going to write a song!"

Berlin jumped out of bed, dashed to his piano, and began composing. The tunes and lyrics seem to flow almost effortlessly, and by 4:00 a.m., he was finished. In less than three hours, he had written a song that would be made famous by Bing Crosby and Rosemary Clooney. The message of the song: "When you're worried and you can't sleep, count your blessings instead of sheep!"

Berlin later recalled that after finishing the song, "I went back to bed—but I still couldn't sleep."

As we come to Esther 6, we find another man suffering from insomnia—Xerxes, the King of Persia. His remedy for sleeplessness is not to write a song but to read a book—and as he reads, the king finds that he too has blessings worth counting!

THE HINGES OF HISTORY

Esther 5 concluded on a note of suspense and impending doom. The villain of this story, Haman the Agagite, is truly a Hitlerian figure—a man of seemingly limitless ego, self-absorption, and cruelty. We have just seen him plot the death of Mordecai by crucifixion, along with the mass murder of the entire population of Jews in Persia.

Now, in Esther 6, the scene shifts and the plot thickens. The very same night that Haman orders the execution of Mordecai, we witness this dramatic scene:

> That night the king could not sleep; so he ordered the book of the chronicles, the record of his reign, to be brought in and read to him. It was found recorded there that Mordecai had exposed Bigthana and Teresh, two of the king's officers who guarded the doorway, who had conspired to assassinate King Xerxes.
>
> "What honor and recognition has Mordecai received for this?" the king asked.
>
> "Nothing has been done for him," his attendants answered (Esther 6:1–3).

The scene opens with a restless and sleepless king. This seems at first to be a rather trivial incident—yet as we shall soon see, the king's insomnia becomes one of those seemingly minor events that turns the hinges of history.

It's amazing how often our lives turn on such seemingly "trivial" factors. A young man and young woman bump elbows in a coffee shop, begin talking, start dating, fall in love, marry, raise a family, and grow old together. But what if they had never bumped elbows? The course of their lives would have been radically different.

In 1962, American Airlines Flight One took off from Idewild (now JFK International) Airport in New York City. Then, just a few miles from the airport, the plane crashed into Jamaica Bay. Ninety-five people died.

After a painstaking investigation, the Federal Aviation Administration determined that the crash was caused by a tiny wire, no more than six inches in length, which had malfunctioned and thrown the rudder askew.

Trivial events often produce major consequences. Here is a king who could not sleep—and because of his insomnia, history would be changed and an untold number of lives would be saved.

You probably know the feeling of lying awake at night, unable to sleep. It's not hard to imagine how this king felt. He lay down, expecting to fall quickly into slumber. But as his mind went over the events of the day, he remembered Queen Esther's curious and perplexing behavior.

Why had she come to him with this strange request? Why had she asked him to come to dinner with her and with Haman, the prime minister? And why, at the risk of her life, did she brave his disfavor in order to speak to him?

Clearly, there was a mystery here. Whatever Queen Esther's hidden purpose might be, it involved matters of extreme importance. Otherwise, she would never have risked everything to speak to him.

King Xerxes tried to put his questions out of his mind, but they kept returning, haunting him, and keeping sleep far from him. He tossed and turned restlessly. In the wee hours of the morning, the king decided to try a common remedy for insomnia: reading a book. Reading often gets our minds off the troubled thoughts that disturb our sleep. So the king sent for the chronicles of the kingdom, the record of his reign.

You might say, "If sleep is what he wants, he certainly picked the right book—the Persian Empire's equivalent of the Congressional Record. What could be more dull? That book could put anyone to sleep!"

But the chronicles of the kingdom were not mere dull accounts—and certainly not to the king! This book was the official record of memorable deeds, of adventure and heroism, of the great accomplishments and glories of the empire. As his attendants read to him, the king was reminded of the story that was summarized in Esther 2:

> During the time Mordecai was sitting at the king's gate, Bigthana
> and Teresh, two of the king's officers who guarded the doorway,
> became angry and conspired to assassinate King Xerxes. But Mordecai

found out about the plot and told Queen Esther, who in turn reported it to the king, giving credit to Mordecai. And when the report was investigated and found to be true, the two officials were hanged on a gallows. All this was recorded in the book of the annals in the presence of the king (Esther 2:21–23).

This had happened five years before the king's sleepless night. Upon being reminded of this event, the king asked what had been done to honor Mordecai. When he found out nothing had been done, the king was astonished and dismayed. Here was a man who had saved the king's life and had prevented a coup d'état—yet he had gone completely unrewarded!

In those ancient days, long before the rise of democracy, palace revolt was a common way to change a government—and it was the scourge and terror of kings. The man who helped avert a palace coup should have been richly rewarded and highly honored! King Xerxes knew he was deeply indebted to Mordecai—he owed this man his life. And an honorable king always repays his debts.

THE DEBT WE OWE

It is a sobering thing to know that you owe your life to another.

In November 1950, President Harry Truman was staying in Blair House, the presidential guesthouse in Washington, while the White House was undergoing renovation. He was upstairs in bed, taking an afternoon nap, when he was awakened by the sound of gunfire in the street below. A pair of radical terrorists was attempting to break into the building and assassinate President Truman.

White House policemen stopped the two gunmen at the entrance and engaged them in a shootout on the street. One of the officers, Leslie William Coffelt, was slain in the attack.

The following day, a somber President Truman said, "It's a strange thing to know that you are alive because another man has died. I will never forget what he has done for me."

If you are a follower of Christ, you are probably aware of the parallel I'm about to draw. You and I, as Christians, know exactly what it feels like to say, "I am alive because another Man has died. I will never forget what He has done for me."

Whenever we open our Bible, we hold in our hands a record of memorable deeds. It is the story of the One who put everything, including life itself, on the line for you and me.

In the pages of that book, we read of the terrible hours when our Lord hung upon the cross, engaged in a death struggle with the powers of darkness. It was the most daring and heroic deed in all human history! There is nothing like it anywhere else in the chronicles of humanity. Nothing compares to the story of this one Man, totally alone, suffering indescribable physical, mental, and spiritual torture while doing battle with the cosmic forces of evil.

He died in our place and for our sake—the Good Shepherd giving His life for the sheep. As Paul wrote, "God made him who had no sin to be sin for us, so that in him we might become the righteousness of God" (2 Corinthians 5:21). When by the Holy Spirit we grasp what Jesus Christ accomplished for us on the cross and that our lives and our hope rest entirely on Him, we realize how much we owe Him.

At the age of six, John Wesley was rescued from a fire in the old rectory where he lived. The boy narrowly escaped with his life. Years later, an artist gave him a drawing of the burning rectory. In the margin beneath the drawing, Wesley wrote with his own hand, quoting Zechariah 3:2, that he was a "brand plucked from the burning."

That is how the great British theologian John Wesley saw himself: A stick snatched from the flames—not merely the flames of the burning rectory but the flames of an eternity without Christ. He kept that drawing throughout his life as a constant reminder of all he owed to the One who gave His life on the cross for John Wesley.

And for you and me.

Have you learned to see yourself that way—as a burning stick snatched from the fire? The apostle Paul tells us, "You are not your own; you were bought at a price" (1 Corinthians 6:19-20). That is where God begins when He seeks to convince us that the flesh is not our friend, but an enemy.

85

What does it mean to be a Christian? It is not simply a matter of agreeing to a set of doctrines or following a set of teachings. It means that the life you live was bought at the price of blood, agony, tears, and death. It is good to remember, as often as possible, what our Lord endured to purchase our salvation. Whenever we recall all that He went through, we discover anew that He has a complete claim to every part of our lives.

Deliverance begins when we truly discover who is our Friend. What a friend we have in Jesus!

THE KING'S DELIGHT

After the king discovers the debt he owes Mordecai, we next see the expression of the king's delight:

> The king said, "Who is in the court?" Now Haman had just entered the outer court of the palace to speak to the king about hanging Mordecai on the gallows he had erected for him.
>
> His attendants answered, "Haman is standing in the court."
>
> "Bring him in," the king ordered.
>
> When Haman entered, the king asked him, "What should be done for the man the king delights to honor?"
>
> Now Haman thought to himself, "Who is there that the king would rather honor than me?" So he answered the king, "For the man the king delights to honor, have them bring a royal robe the king has worn and a horse the king has ridden, one with a royal crest placed on its head. Then let the robe and horse be entrusted to one of the king's most noble princes. Let them robe the man the king delights to honor, and lead him on the horse through the city streets, proclaiming before him, 'This is what is done for the man the king delights to honor!'"
>
> "Go at once," the king commanded Haman. "Get the robe and the horse and do just as you have suggested for Mordecai the Jew, who sits at the king's gate. Do not neglect anything you have recommended."
>
> So Haman got the robe and the horse. He robed Mordecai, and led him on horseback through the city streets, proclaiming before

him, "This is what is done for the man the king delights to honor!" (Esther 6:4–11).

Four times in this account we see the phrase "the man the king delights to honor." Out of the king's recollection of Mordecai's deed comes this great and generous feeling of delight.

Notice how the invisible hand of God (whose name is never mentioned but whose activity is ever-present) arranges these events. Early in the morning, the king hastens to display his gratitude toward Mordecai. He asks who is on duty in the royal court. By a strange twist of fate—one of those coincidences that is *never* a coincidence—Haman has entered the royal court with the intention of proposing his murderous scheme to the king.

But before Haman can set his plan in motion, the king greets Haman with a question: "What should be done for the man the king delights to honor?" So egotistical is Haman that he assumes that the king is referring to Haman himself! This is so typical of the flesh within us—proud, self-absorbed, and arrogant.

The irony of this scene is so delicious we can taste it. Haman knows what true honor is. He knows the kind of honor that he himself lusts for. Without hesitation, Haman gives the king a list of ceremonial tributes that should be paid to the man the king delights to honor. He tells the king to clothe that man in kingly clothes, set him upon the king's own horse, place a kingly crown upon his brow, and send him riding through the streets with a servant shouting a proclamation of his glory: "This is what is done for the man the king delights to honor!"

Notice the symbolism, as it applies to your life and mine: Jesus has said, "My Father will honor the one who serves me" (John 12:26). And the honor God gives is His own kingly honor! God gives us His own clothing, His horse, His crown, and all that He is. That is true honor.

So we have to ask ourselves: Do we honestly desire to honor the One to whom we owe our very lives? How do we honor the One who delights to honor us? The message of the New Testament is that we honor God by returning to Him the honors He has bestowed on us. We give him back the clothes, the horse, the crown, and the words of glory. That is the message Paul underscores again and again to us: "Offer yourselves to God, as those who have been brought from death to life" (Romans 6:13). "Offer your bodies as living sacrifices, holy and pleasing to God" (Romans 12:1). "You were bought at a price. Therefore honor God with your body" (1 Corinthians 6:20).

Is it your delight to do this? If not, then you have forgotten the One to whom you owe your life! Grant Him authority over your life. Give Him your crown to wear. Grant Him the right to be Lord of every aspect of your life! That is true honor.

THE DESPERATION OF THE FLESH

The final scene of Esther 6 reveals what happens to Haman. It is a picture of the utter desperation of the flesh.

> "Go at once," the king commanded Haman. "Get the robe and the horse and do just as you have suggested for Mordecai the Jew, who sits at the king's gate. Do not neglect anything you have recommended."
>
> So Haman got the robe and the horse. He robed Mordecai, and led him on horseback through the city streets, proclaiming before him, "This is what is done for the man the king delights to honor!"
>
> Afterward Mordecai returned to the king's gate. But Haman rushed home, with his head covered in grief, and told Zeresh his wife and all his friends everything that had happened to him.
>
> His advisers and his wife Zeresh said to him, "Since Mordecai, before whom your downfall has started, is of Jewish origin, you cannot stand against him—you will surely come to ruin!" While they were still talking with him, the king's eunuchs arrived and hurried Haman away to the banquet Esther had prepared (Esther 6:10–14).

What a picture of bitter humiliation!

Haman, in a blinding rage, walks through the streets of the city leading Mordecai's horse. All the honors Haman coveted for himself—the royal garments and the crown and the shouts of praise—are now showered on

Haman's worst enemy! And Haman himself is forced to shout Mordecai's praise! Haman's dreams of glory have become a nightmare of humiliation. When his ordeal finally ends, Haman rushes home "with his head covered in grief" (v. 12).

Why did Haman submit to this humiliation? Moments before, he had been planning Mordecai's execution. Now he was praising Mordecai in the streets. Why didn't he simply tell the king he refused to honor Mordecai?

Answer: Haman was committed to surviving. Haman didn't dare refuse an order from the king. To do so was to risk death. So Haman swallowed his pride (which was a lot to swallow!), covered his head with grief and humiliation, and carried out the king's order.

You may have noticed some Haman-like flesh in your own life. When you become earnest and excited about serving Christ, it's easy to honor Him, serve Him, and love Him. But in time, you realize that there are risks to serving Christ. Christians have to take unpopular stands. Christians have to oppose popular opinion and cultural trends. Sometimes it is costly to take a stand for Christ.

So we learn to compromise. There are many ways that we can *look* like we're serving Christ without actually doing so. We can say the right things in the right places at the right times so we can appear pious and spiritual— but without ever having to take a tough stand for Christ. We can appear to be Christians without ever truly taking up our cross and following Him.

This is the flesh, bowing to the demands of the king but only because it is the price of survival to be a "respectable" and "non-threatening" Christian. Left to itself, the flesh is openly arrogant, boastful, lustful, and proud. But when cornered by the Spirit, the flesh adopts a disguise of righteousness and becomes pious, religious, scrupulous about morals, zealous in church work, indignant over wrongs, and obnoxiously "orthodox"!

The righteousness of the flesh is always *counterfeit* righteousness—a self-seeking, self-absorbed self-righteousness. Haman can make a *show* of honoring Mordecai, but there is no sincerity in his heart. The flesh can put on a big religious show, but it cannot please God. As Paul tells us, "They that are in the flesh cannot please God" (Romans 8:8 KJV). The flesh can memorize Scripture, teach Sunday school, distribute tracts, give big donations, preach sermons, and write Christian books! The flesh can even apologize (after a fashion) and suffer for God (with deep sighs of wounded martyrdom), but there is one thing the flesh will never do: It will never surrender!

I once had a pastor friend who was suffering from a growth on his vocal cords. The doctor told him, "You're a non-smoker, so the odds are nine-to-one the growth is benign. If you were a smoker, the odds would be reversed—nine-to-one the growth is malignant."

We all know that one of the leading causes of death in our society is smoking. Before that first puff on that first cigarette, every smoker has heard about the health risks of smoking dozens, if not hundreds, of times. But people still choose to smoke. Why? While it's true that smokers enjoy the stimulant effect of nicotine, I'm convinced that's not the *real* reason they smoke. And I'm sure it's not because they enjoy the taste of burnt leaves on their tongue. For most smokers, I think smoking is a symbol of being a "real man," or a "liberated woman." In other words, it's a symbol of independence and even rebellion.

That demand for complete independence, for the right to rebel against even the rules of good health and good sense, is a manifestation of the flesh. The flesh displays itself in many forms of human behavior—and always to our detriment.

Take, for example, the sin of pride. I have seen men destroy their families, their friendships, their reputations, and their careers rather than yield on a point of pride. I knew a man who destroyed his relationship with his children and drove them out of his house, one by one, because he was harsh, critical, stubborn, and too proud to admit he was ever wrong. He would far rather see all of his children hate him than ever bend his will or give up the fleshly sin of pride.

THE FLESH MUST DIE

Haman—the flesh—will do anything to survive. He will heap praise on his worst enemy (though he will cover his head with grief!). He will carry out the most humiliating orders of the king (though he is mortified through and through). But Haman will never yield.

There is only one thing that can conquer the stubborn, unyielding will of Haman or our own fleshly nature—the cross of Christ. The flesh cannot change; therefore, it must die.

And so it is with Haman. When he rushes home and tells his wife and friends of his humiliation in having to pay honor to his most hated enemy, they tell him, "Since Mordecai, before whom your downfall has started, is of Jewish origin, you cannot stand against him—you will surely come to ruin!"

This is a premonition of Haman's doom. It's a prophecy of the defeat of the flesh within us all.

When you committed your life to Jesus Christ, He entered into you—not merely to give you a ticket for heaven and a "fire escape" from hell. He came into your life to lay hold of that satanic *thing* that possesses you and rears itself against the love and authority of God. He came to tear it out of your life—to rip it out by the roots!

He came to deliver you from the power of the flesh.

The good news of the gospel of Jesus Christ is that the work of delivering you from the flesh and its corruption has already been accomplished. The Haman-like power of your sinful nature has been broken by the cross of Jesus Christ.

Now it is up to you to appropriate the power of the cross, to live joyfully, victoriously, and free as a child of the living God.

8

HAMAN'S LAST SUPPER

Esther 7

I once visited the Harry S. Truman Library and Museum in Independence, Missouri. The former president was still living at the time, and it was said that he frequently went to the library and often greeted visitors in person. So during our visit I hoped we might encounter Mr. Truman himself.

After we finished our tour, I said to one of the attendants, "Has Mr. Truman been here today?"

"Yes," he replied. "Mr. Truman was here this morning, and he said something that was very characteristic. He had forgotten something, and he said to me, 'Why does a man forget so much when he's past seventy?'"

I was instantly struck by the irony of the former president's complaint. Here was a man who couldn't remember—in a building that was built so the world will never forget. The former president's frustration reminded me of a motivation that is common to us all—an instinctive desire to be remembered. We can endure many forms of hurt and loss, but we cannot endure the thought of being forgotten. That is an agony of spirit few of us can sustain.

Yet, as Christians, we know that there is only one event in history that is truly timeless, eternal, and destined never to be forgotten: The cross of Jesus Christ.

The greatest human civilizations eventually crumble to rubble and dust. The Sumerians, the Egyptians, the Minoans, the Greeks, the Romans, the Phoenicians, and the Incans have all passed into history. The British Empire, which once circled the globe, has shrunk to a shadow of its former self. The Soviet Union has collapsed. Someday even the American civilization will be consigned to history.

The earth itself is far from eternal. Even the universe, so vast and seemingly ageless, has been stamped with an expiration date known only to its Creator. Everyone and everything that is, or ever was, or ever will be is doomed to extinction, doomed to be forgotten and consigned to oblivion—unless those human beings are linked to that one timeless and eternal event: The cross of Jesus Christ. This is an unalterable truth, declared by Scripture, confirmed by history.

The crucifixion of our Lord Jesus Christ took place nearly 2,000 years ago outside the city of Jerusalem, yet it is an event that still has an effect in the everyday experience of every follower of Christ. The cross of Christ is the crisis of history. It stands in judgment over every individual life on this planet. That is why we speak of the cross as a timeless event.

The cross of Jesus Christ affected human history long before it occurred in time and space. That Roman instrument of torture and execution was written about, symbolized, and prophesied throughout the pages of the Old Testament, long before the Roman Empire came into being. The sacrifices of the Old Testament were all pictures of the cross of Christ.

That cross has complete authority over the life of every Christian. This daily manifestation of the cross in our lives is what Esther 7 now portrays for us in parable form.

THE KING'S BANQUET AND THE LAST SUPPER

Esther 7 opens with an intimate supper in a private banquet hall where Queen Esther, King Xerxes, and Haman, the scheming prime minister, are gathered. The chapter closes with a man nailed to a tree, writhing and wailing in agony until dead. Here is one of those frequent and timeless foreshadowings of the cross in the Old Testament. As the scene opens, we read:

> So the king and Haman went to dine with Queen Esther, and as they were drinking wine on that second day, the king again asked, "Queen Esther, what is your petition? It will be given you. What is your request? Even up to half the kingdom, it will be granted."

Then Queen Esther answered, "If I have found favor with you, O king, and if it pleases your majesty, grant me my life—this is my petition. And spare my people—this is my request. For I and my people have been sold for destruction and slaughter and annihilation. If we had merely been sold as male and female slaves, I would have kept quiet, because no such distress would justify disturbing the king."

King Xerxes asked Queen Esther, "Who is he? Where is the man who has dared to do such a thing?" (Esther 7:1–5).

Here is a king who is ignorant of what is going on in his own kingdom. This is a picture of your soul and mine. The human soul has the power of free will and choice, but the soul is also characterized by blindness and ignorance. We must make many of our most important decisions while lacking a true understanding of the reality around us—and even the reality within us. The king is a profound symbol of the fundamental and pathetic ignorance of the human soul.

In contrast to the king, we see Queen Esther, who symbolizes the human spirit. She possesses a deep understanding of hidden events because she's been informed by her cousin, the profoundly wise Mordecai. Because Queen Esther knows what is going on behind the scenes, she is empowered to act—and to avert disaster.

Queen Esther pictures for us the regenerate human spirit which, indwelt and taught by the Holy Spirit, is able to recognize the true nature of evil. The regenerate human spirit serves as a beachhead in the human personality from which God moves in our lives to prevent disaster.

Also at this banquet is Haman, a descendent of Agag, the Amalekite, the sworn enemy of God. He is plotting to destroy the people of God and eradicate them entirely from the kingdom of Persia. In the process, he seeks to exalt himself. He is a picture of the corrupt and fleshly self within each of us—that deadly ego that has as its central purpose the exaltation of self. The flesh hates and rejects the authority of God in our lives.

Although the parallels may not be immediately obvious, there are profound similarities between this banquet and the supper that was held in an upper room in Jerusalem the night before Jesus was betrayed. At the Lord's

Last Supper, we see the same three forces that are represented at this Persian banquet: profound ignorance, wise understanding, and fleshly corruption.

Ignorance was represented by the eleven loyal disciples. Like the king, they did not know what was going on. Their hearts were troubled. They were concerned and perplexed. They were full of questions. They were ignorant and unknowing.

Wisdom was represented by Jesus, their Master, the perfect Son of Man. He was indwelt by the Father, filled with the Spirit, fully awake to the danger of the hour. During the night he was betrayed, Jesus moved steadily and unswervingly into the shadow of death.

Fleshly corruption was represented that night by Judas, the traitor. He was intent on fulfilling his own desires, ready to destroy his own Master in exchange for a bag of silver. Like Haman, Judas set events in motion that ultimately ended with his own death on a tree. Scripture records that Judas went out and hanged himself—much as Haman, in a very real sense, "hanged" himself by his own actions.

But the truly momentous death that followed the Lord's Last Supper was the death of Jesus. Within hours, He was nailed to a tree, impaled in agony upon an instrument of torture and execution. There He died for your sake and mine.

HE BECAME SIN

Whenever we encounter a cross in Scripture, it always exists for one purpose and one purpose only: To put a sinful man to death. That is what the cross must do in your life and mine. And that is what the cross of Jesus did. It was an instrument on which a sinful man met death.

Does that shock you? You might say, "But Jesus was not a sinful man! He was the most innocent human being who ever lived." And that's true— but that's not the entire truth.

One of the most amazing sentences in all of Scripture is Paul's statement, "God made him who had no sin to be sin for us, so that in him we might become the righteousness of God," (2 Corinthians 5:21). In other words, the sinless Man became the sinful Man for our sakes. This did not occur in some vague, symbolic sense. Our sinless Lord truly took on the agony and pain of our sin.

On the cross, Jesus became Haman. He took on all that was selfish, cruel, grasping, proud, and corrupt. It was that writhing, disgusting mass of sin that God nailed to the cross and put to death. It was your sin and mine that caused a barrier of darkness and silence to roll over the skies, cutting Jesus off from the Father, causing him to cry out, "My God, my God, why have you forsaken me?" (Matthew 27:46). He became sin, and God put Him to death.

The timeless event of the cross of Christ must become the supreme event in our own lives. The death of Christ, with all of its power to save us and deliver us, is utterly useless to us until we have translated it into our own experience. When we believe in the cross of Christ and when we act on that belief, then the cross becomes true in our personal experience. Only through applying the truth of the cross of Christ to our own lives can we find victory over the self-loving, self-pleasing, self-defending, and totally corrupted flesh that naturally drives our thinking and behavior.

In Esther 7, we find three specific steps we can each take to apply the cross of Christ to our own lives. Through these three steps, we can find deliverance from the corrupt urges and acts of the Haman-like flesh within:

STEP ONE: THE REVELATION OF EVIL

In the first five verses of this chapter, we saw King Xerxes in his ignorance—and we saw Queen Esther reveal to him that someone was plotting against her and her people. So the king asked, "Who is he? Where is the man who has dared to do such a thing?" and in the next verse, Queen Esther revealed the truth about which the king had been completely unaware:

> Esther said, "The adversary and enemy is this vile Haman." Then Haman was terrified before the king and queen (Esther 7:6).

Queen Esther exposed the evil plan of Haman—and Haman was filled with terror. Whenever the evil of the flesh is exposed within us, we shrink in horror. Whenever we catch a glimpse of how our sins look to other people, we are filled with shame and revulsion for what we have done.

We all have fleshly sins that we keep hidden. We hope that those shameful secrets will never be exposed to the light of day. The flesh within us fights like a fiend to defend itself, protect itself, and shield its plans from scrutiny. But when the corruption of our flesh is inevitably exposed, the result is terror—a desperate wish that we could jump into a hole in the ground and pull the hole in after ourselves.

It's a horrible thing to think you are in the right—only to discover that the *real* problem is your own sin, the corrupt flesh within you. You blamed the thoughtlessness of others—then discovered that the problem was your own selfishness. You blamed the anger of others—then discovered that the problem was your own lack of Christian love. You blamed the coldness of others—then discovered that the problem was your own self-pity. You blamed the fickleness of others—then discovered that the problem was your own jealousy.

We always think we are in the right. We force the Spirit of God to chip away at our defensiveness and self-righteousness with the mallet and chisel of trial and conflict. In our pride, we give Him no choice but to show us our inner corruption through painful circumstances. What a shattering experience it is when the Spirit exposes our true reality to ourselves! We want to respond with denial; we want to reject the proof that is right before our eyes. But when the smug and self-righteous veneer is peeled away, the Spirit reveals to us what lurks beneath: Haman, the traitor, the double-dealing foe.

STEP TWO: INNER CONFLICT

The exposure of Haman is followed by an intense conflict within the heart of the king:

> The king got up in a rage, left his wine and went out into the palace garden. But Haman, realizing that the king had already decided his fate, stayed behind to beg Queen Esther for his life (Esther 7:7).

The king knows who his real enemy is. Why does he leave the table and go away to think? What is there to think about? Why doesn't he simply shout, "Off with his head"?

The reason: King Xerxes is struggling with himself. He is angry with Haman—and rightly so. But he is uncertain what to do. After all, Haman is the prime minister. He has deeply entrenched himself in the affairs of the kingdom, and the king knows that any action taken against Haman will upset the whole kingdom. It is a radical act to execute the prime minister.

What's worse, the king knows that he has been duped and manipulated by this snake in human form. This prideful king realizes that he now looks like a complete fool. He has followed the counsel of this deceiver, and he has put his whole kingdom at risk. On Haman's advice, he has issued an edict that requires the death of every Jew in the kingdom. Including his beautiful Queen Esther! What a fool he has been!

How do you feel when you finally see yourself in the wrong? How do you feel when, after years of justifying and defending yourself, you suddenly see that the principle you have been living by is the very source of all your troubles? You know that if you admit you've been wrong, you may have to shed habits, attitudes, behaviors, and possessions that you have built up over the years. You may have to change your career. You may have to confess your sin and ask forgiveness from a number of people. You may have to make amends to those you have wounded. Above all, you will have to swallow your pride.

In that moment of inner struggle, you will be tempted to compromise, to try to smooth over the problem instead of dealing with it in an honest and forceful way. That is the corruption of the flesh, bargaining and pleading and begging for compromise, just as Haman tried to bargain and plead with Queen Esther.

I will never forget the deep struggle in my own life when it dawned on me that a series of troubled relationships in my life was actually my fault, not the fault of the other people. I had been blaming others for their insensitivity, their thoughtlessness, their lack of consideration for my feelings. One day it occurred to me: What if the problem is that I'm overly sensitive and a bit peevish and touchy? What if I make too much of the offhand things people say or the things they don't say that I think they should? In other words, what if *I'm* the problem, not them?

When that realization first occurred to me, I was horrified! I retreated in denial: Oh, no, it can't be *my* fault... can it? I struggled with that thought. I tried to repress it. I tried to rationalize and defend and excuse myself. I didn't want to see my own self-centeredness. I recall spending a full hour in deep inner struggle, remembering all the long hours I had spent in an agony of soul, feeling ill-treated, licking my wounds, and wallowing in self-pity.

And at last I came to the point of acceptance. I said to myself, "All along, the fault was *mine* and no one else's. God has shown me the truth and I must accept it." At that point, the struggle was over.

I am reminded of the story of the rich young ruler who came to Jesus. In just a few sentences of dialogue, the Lord exposed this man's heart and showed him that his love of material possessions had a stranglehold on his soul. Then Jesus said, "Go, sell your possessions and give to the poor, and you will have treasure in heaven. Then come, follow me" (Matthew 19:21).

The rich young ruler went away, full of sorrow, torn and struggling within, wanting to follow Jesus but unwilling to deal with the corruption of the flesh within him. And the Lord, watching him go, was grieved because he loved this young man.

So it is with you and me. It's normal for us to feel conflicted when the corruption and sin of the flesh are exposed in us. The exposure of the flesh always produces conflict. I pray that God will give you the grace, whenever the flesh is exposed in your life, to face it courageously and honestly, to stop defending it, and to put it to death.

STEP THREE: THE DEATH SENTENCE

There is only one way to deal with the flesh: You must pronounce the sentence of death. You cannot compromise with it, bargain with it, or excuse it. You cannot show the flesh any mercy. It must be rooted out of

HAMAN'S LAST SUPPER (*Esther 7*)

your life and destroyed. You must deal with the flesh as King Xerxes dealt with Haman:

> Just as the king returned from the palace garden to the banquet hall, Haman was falling on the couch where Esther was reclining.
>
> The king exclaimed, "Will he even molest the queen while she is with me in the house?"
>
> As soon as the word left the king's mouth, they covered Haman's face. Then Harbona, one of the eunuchs attending the king, said, "A gallows seventy-five feet high stands by Haman's house. He had it made for Mordecai, who spoke up to help the king."
>
> The king said, "Hang him on it!" So they hanged Haman on the gallows he had prepared for Mordecai. Then the king's fury subsided (Esther 7:8–10).

This is like a scene from a Shakespearean drama. The king returns from the garden and finds Haman half-fallen across Queen Esther's couch, clawing at her and cravenly pleading for mercy. The sight of this man with his hands on the queen fills King Xerxes with disgust.

I doubt that Xerxes truly believed that Haman would take that crucial moment to "molest" the queen. He is certainly aware of Haman's terror and desperation. His voice was probably thick with sarcasm as he said, "Will he even molest the queen while she is with me in the house?"

At that moment, one of the attendants of the court reminded the king of the gallows (or execution post) that had been erected for the purpose of torturing Mordecai to death—Mordecai, the man who had saved the king's life!

Reminded of Haman's true character, as exemplified by his plot against Mordecai, the king pronounces the death sentence against Haman: "Hang him on it!"

When the king pronounces his sentence against Haman, the man's evil finally comes to an end. Only when you agree with God that the corrupt flesh deserves death will you find deliverance from the power of the flesh. As Paul tells us, "In the same way, count yourselves dead to sin but alive to God in Christ Jesus" (Romans 6:11).

Crucify the Haman within. Hang him on the cross—and find deliverance.

This is not to say that you can experience a once-and-for-all escape from temptation and sin. While we are here in the body, we will never be free of the attempts of the flesh to drag us back into sin.

But the Haman-like flesh is not stronger than the power of God. Any time we suffer the temptation that comes from the flesh—jealousy, resentment, malice, lust—we can deny Haman the victory. We gain the victory over Haman by recalling that Jesus came and died to put the corrupt flesh within us to death. This is why He became sin for us, so we could say, "Hang it on the cross," and be delivered from sin.

When jealousy burns within you, hang it on the cross. When self-pity tempts you to whine and moan, hang it on the cross. When a critical spirit whispers to you, tempting you to destroy someone's reputation, hang it on the cross. When lust rears its seductive head, hang it on the cross.

Pray, "Lord Jesus, because I see the Haman-like flesh within me as you do, I know it is evil. It wants to destroy your work in my life. I lay my will down alongside yours, Lord, and I agree with you: 'Hang all that is fleshly on the cross! Put it to death! Crucify it!'"

That is the prayer the Haman within you fears most. That is the prayer of victory over the flesh.

9

THE LAW OF THE SPIRIT

Esther 8

*T*he infamous Iraqi dictator Saddam Hussein was born in the village of Tikrit—the same village that gave birth to Saladin, the twelfth-century sultan who ruled all the lands from Syria in the north to Egypt in the south. Just as Saladin led the Muslims against the Crusaders and conquered the Holy Land, Saddam Hussein dreamed of destroying Israel, recapturing Palestine, and conquering the Middle East in his own name. Saddam's ruthless ambition and Iraq's vast oil resources made him a dominant figure on the world scene.

Yet, as an article in the *Atlantic Monthly* once revealed, this self-styled latter-day Saladin was as much a prisoner as he was a ruler:

> Saddam is a loner by nature, and power increases isolation. . . . Responsibility and commitment limit his moves. One might think that the most powerful man has the most choices, but in reality he has the fewest. Too much depends on his every move. . . .
>
> Power gradually shuts the tyrant off from the world. Everything comes to him second or third hand. He is deceived daily. He becomes ignorant of his land, his people, even his own family. He exists, finally, only to preserve his wealth and power, to build his legacy. Survival becomes his one overriding passion. So he regulates his diet, tests his food for poison, exercises behind well-patrolled walls, trusts no one, and tries to control everything.[1]

For a while, Saddam Hussein was the most powerful man in Iraq—and one of the most pathetic figures on the world stage. Despite his power, he was kept in the dark about all the matters he most desperately wanted to control. He was a prisoner of his own power.

King Xerxes was a man like Saddam Hussein in many ways. He was at once powerful and pathetic. So great was the king's power that nothing could be done without his consent—yet he was so naive and ignorant of events around him that he was easily deceived by the crafty Haman into a disastrous decision—a decision that threatened to plunge the Persian Empire into violence and chaos.

INTO THE PRESENCE OF THE KING

As we have seen, this king represents *you*—your soul that rules over the capital city of your body and affects a vast empire of influence, touching everyone who comes in contact with you. The soul is made up of the mind, the emotions, and the will, and all of this is represented by the king in the book of Esther.

Haman, the evil prime minister, represents the sinful nature we have inherited from Adam—a nature which, if not for the revelation of the Bible, we would never know exists. The sinful flesh continually seeks to delude and deceive us, as Haman deceived the king, seducing us into self-effort, self-praise, self-pity, and self-centeredness of every kind.

Deliverance can come to us only through the implantation of a new spirit within us. That new spirit is represented by Queen Esther, who in turn is under the control of the Holy Spirit, represented by Mordecai.

We have traced this story of deliverance to the point where the king's eyes have at last been opened. He now sees the true nature of Haman, and the deception Haman tried to perpetrate has been exposed. The king now sees that his "friend" Haman is truly an enemy. Recognizing the true nature of Haman is the first step toward freeing the kingdom. As we apply these principles to our own lives, we see that recognizing the true nature of our enemy, the flesh, is the first step in achieving spiritual victory through the cross of Christ.

As we come to Esther 8, we trace the steps that follow the decision to put the sinful flesh to death. Those steps begin with a transfer of power and the ascendancy of a new authority:

> That same day King Xerxes gave Queen Esther the estate of Haman, the enemy of the Jews. And Mordecai came into the presence of the king, for Esther had told how he was related to her. The king took off his signet ring, which he had reclaimed from Haman, and presented it to Mordecai. And Esther appointed him over Haman's estate (Esther 8:1–2).

This is the magical moment of the story—a moment full of possibilities. Mordecai has been one of the king's loyal subjects. He saved the king's life by uncovering an assassination plot. He worked behind the scenes, through Esther, to thwart the genocidal plot of Haman. But Mordecai and the king have never met face to face—until now. Finally, Mordecai comes into the presence of the king, and the king responds by giving to Mordecai all that Haman once possessed, including the king's signet ring, the symbol of the office of the prime minister.

Looking at this true story as a parable of our lives, we can see this as the moment when, consciously and deliberately, we reject the authority of self-interest and the flesh, and we yield to the Holy Spirit. This is when we give Him the sovereign right to direct our lives. Since the task of the Holy Spirit is to make the person of Jesus Christ real in our lives, this could also be called the moment when we truly yield ourselves to the lordship of Christ for the very first time.

You may have been a Christian for many years, yet you may never have seen clearly before that God has the right to exercise total authority over every area of your life. There may be parts of your life that you resist turning over to God. It might be your finances. It might be your career goals. It might be the realm of your private thoughts. In some area of your life, you're saying to God, "I let you control certain parts of my life, but I want to keep *this* part of my life under my own control." But the parts of our lives that we withhold from Him are the very areas he wants to intrude into and to talk to us about.

Remember what the Haman-like flesh is? It's the self. In order to truly crucify the flesh, we have to abolish self-interest. Our interests have to align with God's interests. His priorities must become our priorities. We must depose Haman, send him to the gallows, and allow the Spirit of God to take His rightful place as the prime minister of our kingdom.

Some people, when they undergo this experience of crucifying the flesh and yielding themselves fully to God, describe the experience as "a second work of grace" or "the baptism of the Holy Spirit." For some, this new and deeper commitment to Christ is so profound and life-changing that it is like being converted all over again. It feels like a totally new experience, and some people view this new yieldedness as though the Spirit of God were only now entering their lives. But there is a different explanation than all that.

The Spirit has been there all along. The Holy Spirit enters the life of the believer at the moment of conversion. The moment you commit your life to Christ, you are baptized with the Holy Spirit. If you are a Christian, you cannot possess any more of the Spirit than you already have—but the Spirit can always possess more of you! Every time you yield some part of your life that you previously withheld, the Spirit gains even more control of your life.

Although the baptism of the Holy Spirit takes place only once in the Christian life—at the moment of conversion—there is another experience involving the Holy Spirit that is usually repeated again and again throughout the Christian life. That experience is the *filling* of the Holy Spirit. The filling of the Spirit takes place whenever we grant the Spirit His rightful authority over our lives. The moment we discover another area of our lives that is not yet under His control, we need to yield that area over to Him. When we surrender each new area to the Spirit, He fills us anew. So it is possible to have hundreds of fillings of the Spirit over a lifetime.

We see the same principle illustrated for us in Mordecai. He has been a part of the story of Esther from the very beginning. He has been present in the kingdom, but the king had forgotten about him. Then, in the opening verses of chapter 8, Mordecai is brought into the presence of the king. Interpreting this historical story as a parable, we see that this scene symbolizes the moment that the soul becomes conscious of the presence of the Holy Spirit and becomes aware of the need to submit to the Spirit's wisdom and authority.

THE LEGACY OF THE FLESH

Notice also that, although Haman is gone—having been put to death on the tree—the "estate of Haman" still exists: "That same day King Xerxes gave Queen Esther the estate of Haman, the enemy of the Jews. And Esther appointed [Mordecai] over Haman's estate."

The estate of Haman consisted of much more than his house and belongings. The estate also included Haman's household, his family, and all of those sons he was so proud of. The king placed Haman's estate in Esther's hands, and she immediately turned them over to Mordecai, the only one with the wisdom and understanding to handle such a thorny matter.

There is a clear parallel to our own Christian experience. You may have come to a place where you know the truth about the flesh and its corruption. You believe that the cross of Christ has judged the flesh within you, yet you see evidence every day that the flesh still continues to affect and influence you. Haman has been executed, but his household and his sons still remain to stir up trouble and even defeat you.

Our tendency is to try to repress those vestiges of the flesh by willpower alone. Where does the will reside? In the soul.

But notice that in the story the king (who represents the soul) never makes any effort to control or manage the estate of Haman himself. Instead, he turns that problem over to the queen, who symbolizes the human spirit, and he says, "It's your problem, Esther. You deal with it."

And Esther, the spirit, wisely turns the matter over to Mordecai, who represents the Holy Spirit. Esther says, in effect, "Only you have the wisdom to handle this problem. I hereby place you in charge of the estate of Haman." In other words, the human spirit entrusted the legacy and residue of the corrupt flesh to the control of the Holy Spirit.

This is exactly what the New Testament tells us to do. God wants us to recognize that our own willpower is inadequate to the challenge of controlling and defeating the flesh. Instead of battling the flesh, we must simply turn the flesh over to the power of the Holy Spirit. When we place Him in charge, we can simply rest in Him, secure in the knowledge that His infinite wisdom and infinite power are more than a match for the corruption of the flesh.

THE IRREVOCABLE EDICT

One huge problem still remains: The king's edict.

Haman is dead—but before he died, he tricked the king into signing an order of genocide against the Jews. That order threatens not only the Jews but also the stability of the kingdom—and the edict cannot be reversed. The next few verses outline the crisis faced by the king:

> Esther again pleaded with the king, falling at his feet and weeping. She begged him to put an end to the evil plan of Haman the Agagite, which he had devised against the Jews. Then the king extended the gold scepter to Esther and she arose and stood before him.
>
> "If it pleases the king," she said, "and if he regards me with favor and thinks it the right thing to do, and if he is pleased with me, let an order be written overruling the dispatches that Haman son of Hammedatha, the Agagite, devised and wrote to destroy the Jews in all the king's provinces. For how can I bear to see disaster fall on my people? How can I bear to see the destruction of my family?"
>
> King Xerxes replied to Queen Esther and to Mordecai the Jew, "Because Haman attacked the Jews, I have given his estate to Esther, and they have hanged him on the gallows. Now write another decree in the king's name in behalf of the Jews as seems best to you, and seal it with the king's signet ring—for no document written in the king's name and sealed with his ring can be revoked" (Esther 8:3–8).

Here is the law of the Medes and the Persians: The king's decree, written in his name and sealed with his ring, cannot be revoked or altered. The king himself is a prisoner of the law he created. Even though he changes his mind, he cannot change his signed, sealed word. This irrevocable law is also referred to in the book of Daniel: "the laws of the Medes and Persians, which cannot be repealed" (Daniel 6:8, 12).

The unalterable law of the Medes and Persians symbolizes what Paul in Romans calls the law of sin and death, as immutable as the law of gravity. We are born into sin, and the wages of sin is death. The immutability of this law baffles the apostle Paul. He writes:

> So I find this law at work: When I want to do good, evil is right there with me. For in my inner being I delight in God's law; but I see another law at work in the members of my body, waging war against the law of my mind and making me a prisoner of the law of sin at work within my members. What a wretched man I am! Who will rescue me from this body of death? (Romans 7:21–24).

The law of sin and death mocks us. We want to do good, we delight in God's law, but our flesh is at war with our spirit and brings us down in defeat again and again. Even after we have learned of the corrupting power of the flesh, the sinful nature, and even after we stop defending the works of the flesh in our lives (anger, resentment, self-righteousness, pride, and the like), we continue to fail. We thought we could crucify the flesh and be rid of it once and for all, but we can't.

The law of sin is still in force. That is the problem of Paul in Romans 7. So he cries out, "What a wretched man I am! Who will rescue me from this body of death?" This is very much like the cry of Esther as she comes before the king, pleading that he revoke his edict, saying in effect, "Wretched woman that I am, who will deliver my people and me from this law of sin and death that has been proclaimed in the king's name and cannot be revoked?"

The king is helpless! His will is bound by the law of the Medes and Persians. He can only reply, "No document written in the king's name and sealed with his ring can be revoked. I, the most powerful man in the Persian Empire, am powerless to change what I have written. So I place the matter in your hands and Mordecai's. If you, in your wisdom, can find a way out of this dilemma—a solution that does not involve revoking the former decree—then write a new decree in my name, seal it with my ring, and I will agree to it."

REVOKING THE IRREVOCABLE

If the law cannot be revoked, what can be done? The answer: A new law. The next section shows us the wise solution of Mordecai:

> At once the royal secretaries were summoned—on the twenty-third day of the third month, the month of Sivan. They wrote out all Mordecai's orders to the Jews, and to the satraps, governors and nobles of the 127 provinces stretching from India to Cush. These orders were written in the script of each province and the language of each people and also to the Jews in their own script and language. Mordecai wrote in the name of King Xerxes, sealed the dispatches with the king's signet ring, and sent them by mounted couriers, who rode fast horses especially bred for the king.
>
> The king's edict granted the Jews in every city the right to assemble and protect themselves; to destroy, kill and annihilate any armed force of any nationality or province that might attack them and their women and children; and to plunder the property of their enemies. The day appointed for the Jews to do this in all the provinces of King Xerxes was the thirteenth day of the twelfth month, the month of Adar. A copy of the text of the edict was to be issued as law in every province and made known to the people of every nationality so that the Jews would be ready on that day to avenge themselves on their enemies.
>
> The couriers, riding the royal horses, raced out, spurred on by the king's command. And the edict was also issued in the citadel of Susa (Esther 8:9–14).

What is Mordecai's answer to this threat that hangs like the sword of Damocles over the kingdom? He cannot cancel out the old law—but the king has empowered him to write a *new* law, issued with the king's consent. The new law would affect the farthest reaches of the kingdom and would turn the threat of death into victory for the Jews.

Now, considering these events as a parable for our lives, it becomes apparent that our "Mordecai," the Holy Spirit, has accomplished the very same victory for us! Paul writes, ". . . through Christ Jesus the law of the Spirit of life set me free from the law of sin and death" (Romans 8:2). A new law, a new edict, has gone into effect: "I have been crucified with Christ and I no longer live, but Christ lives in me" (Galatians 2:20). The law of His life in me is able to counteract the effects of the law of sin and death. It is no longer I who carries on this struggle. Instead, I allow Him to live His life through me. I still live this life, but "the life I live in the body, I live by faith in the Son of God, who loved me and gave himself for me" (v. 20).

When I rest on Him and count on His indwelling life to work through me, He turns even my failures into victories. The law of the Spirit turns sorrow into celebration, adversity into adventure, and persecution into praise. This new law does not always change our circumstances. But it uses our circumstances and even reverses their effect. The beautiful spiritual paradox of the law of the Spirit is that it is most effective and powerful when we are at our weakest—and even when we are in defeat.

This is the principle Paul discovered through his so-called "thorn in the flesh," a chronic and debilitating affliction that caused him great suffering throughout his ministry. Paul never disclosed what that "thorn in the flesh" was, but he did tell us that he set aside three special times of praying and pleading with God, asking Him to remove that thorn from his life. The Lord's answer to Paul was, "My grace is sufficient for you, for my power is made perfect in weakness" (2 Corinthians 12:9). When we are weak, He is strong.

So the law of the Spirit sets us free from the law of sin and death. We do not need to suffer defeat. We do not need to suffer despair. Even though our circumstances may not change, His indwelling life in us is sufficient to meet every challenge that comes our way.

When the nation of Israel faced defeat at the hands of the Philistines, the law of the Spirit took charge of the situation, operating through a shepherd lad named David. The entire camp of Israel was in despair. Goliath, the Philistine warlord, seemed invincible. But David's faith in an indwelling, all-powerful God transformed pessimism into victory. Although David was just a boy, he stepped up on the battlefield and shouted, "Who is this uncircumcised Philistine that he should defy the armies of the living God?" (1 Samuel 17:26).

There was nothing wrong with David's eyesight. He could see how Goliath towered over him, seemingly invincible. But David didn't look at Goliath through the eyes of the flesh but through the eyes of faith. He saw a Power that towered over even Goliath—the living God of Israel, who was able to meet any circumstance and transform despair into victory. David went up against Goliath, and God, working through the faith of this boy, felled Goliath and gave the victory to David and the nation of Israel.

"ALL IS WELL"

A Christian surgeon once told me about going out with a fellow doctor, a non-Christian, to visit a sick old man who was living alone in a trailer. When the doctors arrived, they found the man sleeping. His body was so riddled with cancer that tumors were breaking out on his scalp. My surgeon friend woke him and said, "How are you doing?"

The old man looked up at them, smiled, and said, "All is well."

They visited with the man for a while, and the man was pleasant and cheerful throughout the visit.

As the two physicians left the trailer, the non-Christian said to my friend, "What does he mean, 'All is well'? Doesn't he know he's dying of cancer? Doesn't he know there's no hope for him?"

My friend replied, "Yes, he knows. But he has a reason to be cheerful. He believes that after this life is over, he'll pass into eternity where there is no cancer and no death. He's not afraid of dying. His faith has overcome his fear of death, and he's ready for whatever comes next. Death isn't defeat for that man; death is victory."

Although the law of death is irrevocable, this man's faith in God enabled him to rise up in victory over that law. Even an "irrevocable" law can be overcome. You don't have to repeal it. You simply need to apply a *different* law to the situation.

There is a natural law that we are all familiar with—the law of gravity, the force of attraction that causes all objects to fall toward the earth. Yet, despite the law of gravity, birds, bees, and airplanes fly. How is that so? Isn't the law of gravity irrevocable?

Yes, it is. But there is another law—the law of aerodynamics, which describes how the motion of air over various surfaces (wings, ailerons, rudders) can enable an airplane to ascend, descend, bank, and turn. The law of gravity is not revoked when an airplane flies—it is still in full force. But the law of aerodynamics enables us to do what the law of gravity says we cannot do: It permits us to fly.

When I board a commercial jet to fly to some other city, I don't tell my wife, "Dear, I'm going aboard this airplane, but I promise that all the way to my destination I'll pull up on the armrests and focus on the problem of conquering gravity. I promise I'll strain and struggle to keep the plane aloft." If I said that, she wouldn't let me go!

The good news is that we don't have to struggle to defeat gravity. The law of aerodynamics has done it for us. All we have to do is sit in the airplane and rest while the plane does all the work.

So it is with the law of sin and death. It's not our job to strain and struggle to defeat that law of death—and it is impossible to do so. The law is irrevocable. But thanks be to God, He has proclaimed a second law, the law of the Spirit. The law of sin and death remains in force, but the law of the Spirit enables us to do what the law of sin and death says is impossible: Through faith in Christ, we can put the flesh to death, we can triumph over temptation and despair, and we can live forever with Him.

A JOYOUS CELEBRATION

The proclamation of the new law changed everything throughout the Persian Empire:

> Mordecai left the king's presence wearing royal garments of blue and white, a large crown of gold and a purple robe of fine linen. And the city of Susa held a joyous celebration. For the Jews it was a time of happiness and joy, gladness and honor. In every province and

in every city, wherever the edict of the king went, there was joy and gladness among the Jews, with feasting and celebrating. And many people of other nationalities became Jews because fear of the Jews had seized them (Esther 8:15–17).

There is joy and celebration among the Jews—even though their deliverance has not yet taken place. Why? Everything has changed for them because of the realization that *victory is finally possible.*

After the first proclamation, the future of the Jews was a blank wall of death and despair. But the good news of the second proclamation brought instant joy to their defeated hearts. God had made a way out of death and defeat.

Esther 3:12 tells us that the first proclamation was written by Haman himself and sealed in the king's name by the ring that King Xerxes had given him. But the second proclamation was written by Mordecai and sealed in the king's name by that same ring of authority. Thus, the law of the Spirit cancels the law of the flesh—and the result is rejoicing and celebration. This speaks to the great sense of joy and relief we feel when the truth of the law of the Spirit breaks upon our despairing hearts. God does not always make a way out of our circumstances, but he always makes a way out of defeat.

During World War II, I was in the United States Navy serving in Pearl Harbor. I worked at the Ships Service Department, the department store for the Navy, and a watch was posted there all night long. My turn came to take the four-hour night watch, which lasted from 2:00 a.m. to 6:00 a.m. It was not a difficult assignment. I could read and write letters and otherwise occupy myself—as long as I didn't go to sleep. During that watch, I read from a book called *Romans: Verse by Verse* by William R. Newell. As I read, I encountered this verse:

> "For sin shall not be your master, because you are not under law, but under grace" (Romans 6:14).

I had read that verse many times before, but this time it seemed to leap off the page. It was like a thing alive, and it thundered to me: "Sin shall not be your master!" I had been wrestling with problems in my life over which I could find no victory, and I was nearing the point of despair. But that sentence shouted to me, filling me with joy and a sense of excitement. I didn't know how it would work out yet, but I knew that my faith had latched onto something powerful: "Sin shall not—*shall not*—SHALL NOT—be your master!" Through the ensuing years, the Lord fulfilled that promise and the things that had held me in bondage are now broken and defeated.

But the sense of excitement and rejoicing came at the moment I knew that victory was possible.

PREPARED TO GIVE AN ANSWER

We see another amazing result of the second edict. Not only is there great joy among the Jews but there is also tremendous convicting power among the non-Jews living in Persia:

> And many people of other nationalities became Jews because fear of the Jews had seized them (Esther 8:17).

Gentiles became Jews! People of many nationalities across the far-flung Persian Empire adopted the principles and practices of the people of God. They abandoned their pagan idols and turned to the one true God.

What parallels do you see to your own life?

When your way of life becomes perceptibly different from the ways of the culture around you, other people notice the difference. They are struck by the fact that you don't think, talk, and act like a pagan. There is something different about you. It's an attractive difference—the fragrance of Christ in your life.

When you respond to trials, opposition, and mistreatment with Christlike grace, other people want to know what you possess that they don't have. This gives you a chance to share with others the difference Christ has made in your life. As the apostle Peter wrote, "Always be prepared to give an answer to everyone who asks you to give the reason for the hope that you have" (1 Peter 3:15). When your life cannot be explained in terms of your human personality, when you display a hope and a peace that passes human understanding, you have an opportunity to share your faith and hope with others—and that is the most powerful Christian witness of all.

A man once told me, "I used to have a very low opinion of Christianity and churches. But I've had a chance to get to know a number of people in your church, and they have transformed my attitude toward the Christian faith. I can't quite put my finger on it, but there's *something* different about the people in your church."

I was delighted to hear this—and I think the Lord himself was even more delighted. As the troubles and crises of this world begin to intensify and multiply, we have a chance to show the world what Christians are made of. The law of the Spirit turns fear into faith, despair into hope, hurt into healing, crisis into opportunity, and defeat into victory. No matter how dark this world becomes, the darkness can never overcome the light of Christ within us.

10

THE SWEET TASTE
OF VICTORY

Esther 9:1–15

*I*n 47 BC, Roman emperor Julius Caesar returned home after defeating Pharnaces II, king of Pontus, at Zela in Asia Minor. Standing before cheering crowds in Rome, he announced, "*Veni, vidi, vici*"—I came, I saw, I conquered.

More than 1,700 years later, John III Sobieski, the king of Poland, led his army to triumph over the invading Turkish forces. Afterwards, he announced his victory: "I came, I saw—God conquered."

We come now to Esther 9, the actual moment of victory for the Jewish people in Persia. It is not a victory any human being can take credit for; we have to stand in amazement and say, "God conquered." This victory brings glory to God, even though He is not named in this account.

As we are about to see, the account of this stunning victory fills only half of one chapter—yet it takes all of the complex, interwoven events of the preceding eight chapters of Esther to bring this victory about. This story is much like an iceberg, which hides nine-tenths of its bulk beneath the surface of the water. The climactic battle of Esther 9 is just the tip of the iceberg of this story. The great victory of the Jewish people in this chapter is a small part of the intricate plan that God has been weaving throughout the book of Esther.

And the same is true of your life and mine. The moment of victory and deliverance in our lives may only be the final ten percent of the story, the merest tip of the iceberg. But God is at work in our lives, weaving together thousands of details and events to bring us to the place of victory. As we witness the triumphant climax of this drama—as we look closely—we will discern echoes of our own life-drama in its pages.

THE APPOINTED DAY

Throughout the book of Esther, the clock has been counting down toward an appointed time. The king's first edict is a ticking time bomb, waiting to explode:

> On the thirteenth day of the twelfth month, the month of Adar, the edict commanded by the king was to be carried out. On this day the enemies of the Jews had hoped to overpower them, but now the tables were turned and the Jews got the upper hand over those who hated them. The Jews assembled in their cities in all the provinces of King Xerxes to attack those seeking their destruction. No one could stand against them, because the people of all the other nationalities were afraid of them (Esther 9:1–2).

The day has come—the day the unbending law of the Medes and the Persians has established for the slaughter of the Jews. But there is a second law in force, and it too cannot be revoked. These two iron-fisted laws are destined to clash head-on at the same moment in history. One law demands the extermination of the Jews. The other permits the Jews to destroy their foes.

When God teaches us an important truth, He always appoints a time when we put that truth to the test. It's easy to go to church or a Bible study and learn exciting, marvelous truths from God's Word. But the Christian life is not just a classroom. It's also a testing ground. The lessons we learn from His Word must eventually be field-tested in the trenches of everyday living. God never imparts a lesson without appointing a day for us to test that lesson in the pressure cooker of everyday experience.

We see this principle at work in the interaction between Jesus and His disciples. In Mark 4, we see Jesus teaching crowds of people by the Sea of Galilee. He teaches them through one parable after another, such as the parable of the sower and the parable of the mustard seed. What are these parables about? Faith! Jesus is teaching the crowds—and His disciples— what it means to have faith.

That same evening, the Lord takes the disciples down to the shore, points to a boat, and says, "Let us go over to the other side." So He and the disciples get in the boat and make their way toward the far shore of the Sea of Galilee. As they are sailing at night, a furious storm whips up, and the waves threaten to swamp the boat. The boat is in danger of sinking—yet Jesus sleeps soundly in the stern of the boat.

The disciples wake him and say, "Teacher, don't you care if we drown?" Remember, these were fishermen. They had seen storms before—but this was terrifying. These men were sure they were about to die.

Jesus arose, rebuked the storm—and the wind and waves instantly subsided. Then He turned and said to His disciples, "Why are you so afraid? Do you still have no faith?"

All day long, Jesus had taught these men about faith. They had sat in his open-air "classroom" on the hillside, and He had taught them lesson after lesson, parable after parable, on what it means to have faith in God. Then He took them out into the storm and tested what they had learned.

Until their faith was tested, these men probably thought they knew what faith really was. But when the storm came up, they discovered they had a lot to learn about faith—and about this amazing Man they called Master and Teacher.

You may have found this same principle at work in your own life. You read the words of Scripture, and God speaks to your heart. You say, "Oh, this is a wonderful new insight! God has opened my eyes to a profound truth." And you think you've mastered it—until the appointed day of testing arrives.

Suddenly you discover that you still have much to learn about faith or about patience or about forgiveness or about some other deep truth of the Christian life.

Throughout the book of Esther, God has been teaching King Xerxes, Queen Esther, and all the Jewish people about His perfect plan for them. He has been teaching them truths about His dependability, even in a time of crisis, a time of seeming hopelessness and despair. Now the appointed time has come when He will put His truth to the test in their lives.

THE EPIC BATTLE BEGINS

Next, we read of the pattern of victory that the Jews experienced on the appointed day of testing:

> The Jews assembled in their cities in all the provinces of King Xerxes to attack those seeking their destruction. No one could stand against them, because the people of all the other nationalities were afraid of them. And all the nobles of the provinces, the satraps, the governors and the king's administrators helped the Jews, because fear of Mordecai had seized them. Mordecai was prominent in the palace; his reputation spread throughout the provinces, and he became more and more powerful.
>
> The Jews struck down all their enemies with the sword, killing and destroying them, and they did what they pleased to those who hated them. In the citadel of Susa, the Jews killed and destroyed five hundred men. They also killed Parshandatha, Dalphon, Aspatha, Poratha, Adalia, Aridatha, Parmashta, Arisai, Aridai and Vaizatha, the ten sons of Haman son of Hammedatha, the enemy of the Jews. But they did not lay their hands on the plunder (Esther 9:2–10).

This epic battle is the climactic turning point in the story of Esther.

The Jews have many bloodthirsty enemies throughout the Persian Empire. Literally hundreds of cruel Persian warriors are sharpening their swords, eager to carry out the king's first edict.

The drama begins to unfold with the new edict from the king—an edict that gives the Jews the freedom to defend themselves. The old edict, drafted by Haman, had given the enemies of the Jews the full legal right to kill the Jews, slaughter their families, and seize their property with the full blessing and approval of the Persian Empire.

But the new edict, written by Mordecai, declares that on the same day appointed for the slaughter of the Jews, the Jews will be permitted to defend themselves. Under the first edict, the Jews would surely have defended themselves anyway—but the law of the Persian Empire would have been against them. Even if they had successfully fended of one or two attacks, they could not hold out forever. The forces of the Empire were stacked against them. They would have been treated as outlaws and rebels against the law of the land, and they could never hope to prevail.

The second edict changed all of that. Now they were permitted to fight for their lives, their families, and their property—and this right was backed by the full authority of the king himself.

THE OLD LAW AND THE NEW LAW

Do you see what these two edicts picture for us? They answer the troubling question raised in Paul's letter to the Romans: What place does the Old Testament law have in the life of a follower of Christ? In Romans 7, Paul writes:

> For when we were controlled by the sinful nature, the sinful passions aroused by the law were at work in our bodies, so that we bore fruit for death. But now, by dying to what once bound us, we have been released from the law so that we serve in the new way of the Spirit, and not in the old way of the written code (Romans 7:5–6).

Here Paul contrasts the Old Testament law, the old written code, against the new way of the Spirit. Here's a direct parallel with the two edicts of the king in the book of Esther. The first edict permitted (indeed, commanded) the enemies of the Jews to attack the Jews on that particular day and spread death throughout the country. The first edict aroused passions of murder, cruelty, and greed, just as Paul said the Old Testament law aroused our sinful passions. So the Old Testament law brings forth death, just as the first edict brings forth death.

But just as the second edict changes everything, so does the new way of the Spirit change everything. Paul tells us that a new law has gone forth, the way of the Spirit of new life in Christ, which sets us free from the condemnation of the old law. Now we are free to fight in the name of God—and we are free to overcome our spiritual enemies (the temptation of Satan and the corrupting influence of the flesh). The new law enables us to experience true victory.

Notice that "all the nobles of the provinces, the satraps, the governors and the king's administrators" now assemble to help the Jews in their fight against their enemies. Isn't this remarkable? The very people who would have enforced the first edict against the Jews now rise up and stand with the Jews in their struggle. This unexpected help arises purely as a result of the second edict.

Again, we see a revelation of truth that we can apply to our everyday lives. The emergence of help from an unexpected source tells us that even when our circumstances are against us and hold us in bondage, forces will come to our aid in ways we do not expect. Indeed, forces that once seemed arrayed against us will become our allies in the battle.

Remember the experience of the Old Testament hero Joseph? His brothers sold him into slavery, and he ended up in prison for a crime he did not commit. But God did not forget him, and years later he rose to the highest position in the government of Egypt, next to Pharaoh himself. In time, Joseph's brothers came to Egypt for help because of a famine in the land of Canaan. The brothers met with Joseph, not realizing that this "Egyptian" leader was actually their own long-lost brother. He revealed himself to them, and in their guilt, they feared for their lives.

Then Joseph spoke these wonderful words: "You intended to harm me, but God intended it for good to accomplish what is now being done, the saving of many lives" (Genesis 50:20). The very circumstances that had placed Joseph in bondage and in prison were used by God to bring him to a place of exaltation—a place where he could be reunited and unified with his father and brothers once more.

And so it is with you and me. The very obstacles and opposition we face in life, the people and events that seem bent on doing us harm, are being used by God to accomplish His good purpose in our lives. The forces that seemed arrayed against us under the old law will become our allies under the way of the Spirit.

As I have read through the book of Acts, I have often wondered what the Christians at Damascus must have thought when the newly converted

Saul of Tarsus arrived in their city. Prior to his conversion, Saul was a first-century believer's worst nightmare. He threatened and arrested Christians, taking whole families into custody and dragging them off in chains.

But after his encounter with the risen Christ on the road to Damascus, he was blinded and shaken. He had to be led around by the hand. Many Christians in Damascus were afraid to trust him, afraid that this was some sort of ruse he was using to capture even more Christians and imprison them for their beliefs.

But as time passed, it became clear that Saul's conversion was genuine. Those who had been hiding in fear of their lives now embraced Saul (who would soon be known as the apostle Paul). He became their dearest friend and ally. God had arrested the arrestor and captured the captor. He transformed the greatest enemy of the church into its most ardent defender.

That is the victory God has planned for each of us. He will transform our opponents into allies, and we will receive aid in our battle from completely unexpected sources.

A MIGHTY WIND

Next, we see that not only did the Jews have the freedom to fight but they were also given the power to fight. That power came from Mordecai himself. As verse 4 tells us, "Mordecai was prominent in the palace; his reputation spread throughout the provinces, and he became more and more powerful."

When the Jews fought against their opponents, they were encouraged by the fact that the man of power was on their side. Mordecai himself stood next to the throne of King Xerxes, so that they had not only the authority to fight back against their enemies but they also had the power of the throne behind them. They battled in total dependence on that power.

Remember that throughout the book of Esther, Mordecai is a picture of the Holy Spirit at work in your life and mine. So, in view of the parallels for our own lives, we see that we have been given the power of the Holy Spirit to fight our spiritual enemies, both Satan and the flesh.

I once saw a magazine photo of a straw—a thin, dry stalk of a cereal plant—that was picked up by a tornado and driven like a nail into a telephone pole. One end of that thin little stalk was buried inches deep into the pole. How is that possible? You couldn't drive a straw through a pole with a hammer. So how do you explain that photo?

There is only one answer: That weak and spindly straw was caught up in the power of the tornado. The indescribable strength of the mighty wind was able to do that which human strength could never do—drive a straw into a wooden pole. It's no coincidence that, throughout the Scriptures, the Spirit of God is pictured as a mighty wind, the breath of God. Again and again, throughout the Bible, this is the image of His ministry in our lives.

God has set us free from the law by the presence of a new life within us—the life of Jesus Christ. His life is continually ministered to us by the Holy Spirit. The Spirit gives us just the kind of power we need for every situation in life. He will never send us a tornado if all we need is a gentle breeze. But if the times call for a tornado, then expect a tornado! He can move mountains, topple kingdoms, and change the course of history. He has sovereign control over your life and mine, and He gives us the victory in every battle we face.

STAND YOUR GROUND AND FIGHT!

The Jews in Persia received the freedom and power to fight. And when the moment came, they fought! We read:

> The Jews struck down all their enemies with the sword, killing
> and destroying them, and they did what they pleased to those who
> hated them (Esther 9:5).

God created all the conditions for victory. He caused the second edict to be issued. He placed Mordecai in a position of power, giving the Jews the legal authority to fight. But everything God did to prepare them for victory would have been wasted if they had not proceeded to draw their swords and fight.

This is the point where many Christians fail to apply truth to experience. I have heard Christians ask, "What should I do when I come up against a moment of temptation?" When people struggle with temptation, it's not enough to simply tell them, "Just look to the Lord and let God handle your temptation." No, we have to tell them to fight!

God has prepared the way to victory. He has given us the freedom to fight temptation. He has given us the power to fight temptation. But still we have to fight! When we fight, God wins the victory over temptation in us and through us.

There is a very real battle raging within each of us. The path to victory lies in standing on the promise God has given us and refusing to be moved from that position. That's why Paul tells us in Ephesians:

> Finally, be strong in the Lord and in his mighty power. Put on the full armor of God so that you can take your stand against the devil's schemes. For our struggle is not against flesh and blood, but against the rulers, against the authorities, against the powers of this dark world and against the spiritual forces of evil in the heavenly realms. Therefore put on the full armor of God, so that when the day of evil comes, you may be able to stand your ground, and after you have done everything, to stand (Ephesians 6:10–13).

God gives us the strength and the power. He gives us the armor of His protection. But we have to put on the armor. We have to draw our sword. We have to stand our ground. We have to fight the fight and actively seize the victory that God has given us in Jesus Christ.

Remember the struggle of our Lord in the Garden of Gethsemane? He could not simply turn His struggle over to the Father. His entire being was a battlefield as He prayed for the strength to endure what lay ahead. The mental anguish and spiritual pressure of that struggle caused the blood to be squeezed from his veins, dropping to the ground like sweat. He prayed for some way out of that horrible ordeal, yet He stood His ground. He refused to be moved. He fought.

In that struggle, He won the victory over Satan. As the apostle James says to us, "Submit yourselves, then, to God. Resist the devil, and he will flee from you" (James 4:7). It's not enough merely to submit to God. It's not enough merely to resist temptation. We must do both! We must submit to God, accepting the preparation He has made for victory; and we must act, we must resist the devil, we must fight the battle. Only by both submitting to God and resisting Satan can we win the victory as God intends.

It's useless to try to resist the devil if you have never submitted yourself to God. That is a prescription for defeat. Stand and fight—but make sure you fight in the strength of God, in the power of God, by the authority of God. Stand your ground—the ground of faith.

VICTORY OVER THE SELF

Next, it's important to see the intensely personal nature of this fight. Ten of the most hateful enemies of the Jews are identified for us in the next few verses:

> In the citadel of Susa, the Jews killed and destroyed five hundred men. They also killed Parshandatha, Dalphon, Aspatha, Poratha, Adalia, Aridatha, Parmashta, Arisai, Aridai and Vaizatha, the ten sons of Haman son of Hammedatha, the enemy of the Jews. But they did not lay their hands on the plunder (Esther 9:6–10).

These ten hateful enemies were the ten sons of Haman. They are listed for us by name. In studying these names, I found that in the original Hebrew language, the ten sons are listed in a peculiar fashion. To each of these names the Hebrew word for *self* is attached. The names are written in a parallel column, and on the opposite column, the word *self* is repeated after each name. I tried to discover the meaning of these names, because names that are listed in the Hebrew Scriptures are often significant. I was able to find the meaning for eight of the names, but two of them I was unable to track down. Here are the names and their meaning:

Parshandatha means "curious-self." If we take these names to be descriptions of the character and personality qualities of these sons of Haman, then Parshandatha's name suggests that he was nosy—that he would pry into other people's business. Perhaps he even spied on people and was one of the resources Haman relied on to keep tabs on potential enemies—maybe even the king.

Dalphon means "weeping-self." His name suggests that he was prone to self-pity and self-absorption. Rich and spoiled, he probably felt sorry for himself anytime he didn't get his way.

Poratha means "squandering-self." He was a spendthrift, a high roller, characterized by lavish and wasteful spending and possibly gambling. Money ran through his fingers like water.

Aridatha means "strong-self." He was aggressive, assertive, and he never let anyone stand in his way. He cared for no interests but his own.

Parmashta means "preeminent-self." He was ambitious and always "looking out for number one." Like his father, he was narcissistic and self-important.

Arisai means "bold-self." This son of Haman was impudent and insolent. He had no respect for anyone but himself.

Aridai means "dignified-self." This son was characterized by arrogant pride. He walked around with his nose in the air, looking down on everyone around him.

Vaizatha means "pure-self." He was self-righteous and saw himself as better than everyone else around him. He saw himself as "pure" while everyone else was, in his opinion, lowly and polluted.

Although I was unable to find meanings for the names of *Aspatha* and *Adalia*, their names were also connected with the word *self*. Although we don't know exactly how their self-centeredness was manifested, we know that these two men, like their brothers, were as selfish and arrogant as their father.

These ten sons undoubtedly wished to avenge the humiliating and agonizing death of their father Haman. They all set out on the appointed day to unleash their rage and take their revenge. In the end, it was the Jews who wreaked retribution against the ten sons of Haman.

With their deaths, the pattern of victory was complete.

THREE MARKS OF GENUINE VICTORY

The victory described in Esther 9 is a *genuine* victory. This is very different from what many of us call "victory." As Christians, we often settle for an *imitation* victory. We paste on a smile and pretend we are living in triumph over our circumstances. We adjust our halos and pretend to be patient while inwardly we seethe with anxiety, agitation, and restlessness. Or we pretend to be humble and gracious while inwardly struggling with ambition and pride in the desire for preeminence. That is imitation victory. That is a sham and a facade.

There are certain signs of genuine victory—signs that can seem to indicate that God's victory has been manifested in the life of a Christian. As we look at the next few verses, we can see how those signs can be seen in this story.

> The number of those slain in the citadel of Susa was reported to the king that same day. The king said to Queen Esther, "The Jews have killed and destroyed five hundred men and the ten sons of Haman in the citadel of Susa. What have they done in the rest of the king's provinces? Now what is your petition? It will be given you. What is your request? It will also be granted."
>
> "If it pleases the king," Esther answered, "give the Jews in Susa permission to carry out this day's edict tomorrow also, and let Haman's ten sons be hanged on gallows."
>
> So the king commanded that this be done. An edict was issued in Susa, and they hanged the ten sons of Haman. The Jews in Susa came together on the fourteenth day of the month of Adar, and they put to death in Susa three hundred men, but they did not lay their hands on the plunder (Esther 9:11–15).

We can find three features to this story that can help us to understand the concept of genuine victory.

First, there was a double victory in the capital city. The day of victory was extended in the capital to cover a second day.

The Persian Empire can be seen as a picture for us of the wide circle of our influence. In this image Susa, the capital city, represents our own life. In the capital city of Susa, we see a double victory. On the first day and on the second day of the battle, the enemies of the Jews were vanquished.

There is great symbolic significance of this double victory for your life and mine. When you experience God's deliverance, it means so much more to you than it means to anyone else. For example, if God delivers you from the sinful habits of jealousy, impatience, or pride, the people around you may notice that you have become a much more pleasant person. You are much nicer to live with.

But you know that your deliverance goes much deeper than simply being "nice." You feel an incredible sense of release and victory. The Spirit of God has been manifested within the citadel, the capital city of your heart. You once felt bound and imprisoned by your emotions and fleshly thoughts. Now you are free! And that deep sense of freedom means more to you than it ever could to anyone around you.

Second, Esther requested that the ten sons of Haman, who had been killed the day before, now be publicly displayed. Perhaps this can be seen as another sign of victory: The public display of the victory God has achieved in our lives.

Many times, when I have attended men's conferences, I have sat in a gathering of Christian men as they shared about the work God has done in their lives. One man will open his heart and talk about his struggle with impatience toward his wife and kids, and he will tell how God has given him victory over that struggle. Another man will describe how God enabled him to lay to rest feelings of jealousy and lust. Another will say that God has given him victory over the temptation to cut ethical corners in his business. What are these men doing? They are publicly displaying their victory over sin as an encouragement to others.

Third, the passage tells us that the Jews "did not lay their hands on the plunder." That is, the Jews did not seek to enrich themselves through the difficult act of dispatching their enemies. They did only what they had to do and no more. Greed and plunder were not motivating factors—only righteous self-defense. One unmistakable mark of genuine spiritual victory is that we reject worldly greed and ambition.

I have known people who wish to be free of certain temptations and sinful habits in their lives because it will mean a better chance for advancement in the world, or it would make their life easier in some way. In other words, they want victory over the flesh so they can obtain their share of the plunder.

The mark of genuine victory is that you wish to gain victory over sin and the flesh out of obedience to and honor of God. You don't care about grabbing a share of the plunder. When I see a person with an unselfish attitude, I know that the Holy Spirit has genuinely done a work of grace in that person's life.

I once heard a young father tell the story of his little girl's illness. As she became more and more sick, he prayed and bargained with God, saying, "Lord, if you make my little girl well, I will serve you. I'll do anything you say." Finally, as his little girl lay near the point of death, he realized what was wrong with his prayers, and he began praying a new prayer: "Lord, whether you make her well or not, I will serve you. I will do anything you say." That is real victory. That is the mark of a believer who has gained true victory over the self.

Has God set you free from the ambitions and habits and sins that have enslaved you? Has He shown you the pathway to victory over the manifestations of the flesh—sins of bitterness, resentment, jealousy, pride, lust, and all the rest? If so, the proof of authentic victory in your life will be that you no longer seek to gain advantage for yourself. You will seek only to please God and advance His plan for victory in the world.

As the apostle Paul once wrote amid the pressures of persecution, opposition, peril, frustration, and hardship: "But thanks be to God, who always leads us in triumphal procession in Christ and through us spreads everywhere the fragrance of the knowledge of him" (2 Corinthians 2:14). That is the sweet taste of victory for your life and mine.

11

A DAY TO REMEMBER

Esther 9:16–10:3

*E*very year, on the fourteenth day of the Hebrew month of Adar, Jews around the world celebrate the Feast of Purim—a one-day holiday of feasting and joy. This feast commemorates the events in the story of Esther, and it is celebrated by a public reading of the entire book of Esther, by the giving of gifts, by committing acts of charity, and by enjoying a feast called the *Se'udat Purim*. The Feast of Purim is one of the favorite holidays of Jewish children because it is filled with excitement, fun, and noise making.

During the public reading of the book of Esther, people in the audience hold drums or noisemakers called *ra'ashan*. Whenever the name of Haman is mentioned, the people twirl the ra'ashan or pound on the drums to blot out the name of evil. Those who have no noisemakers simply boo or hiss.

The Feast of Purim is celebrated to this day so Jewish people will remember that God delivered them from slaughter in Persia some 500 years before Christ. It is an important day on the Jewish calendar and in Jewish history.

As we come to the closing events in the book of Esther, you may think that the exciting part of the story is over and the rest is anticlimactic. But this last section of the book serves an important purpose. It is designed to teach us the need to remember.

As we have journeyed through the book of Esther, we have seen these events as parables of our own lives. With every aspect of this story, we can make a spiritual application to our own Christian experience today. Once we have been delivered from the way of the flesh and have begun living by the way of the Spirit, there are four key truths that God wants us never to forget.

FIRST KEY TRUTH:
REMEMBER THE FRUIT OF VICTORY

The first truth the Lord wants us never to forget is *the fruit of victory*—the blessed and happy result that victory brings to our lives. We read:

> This happened on the thirteenth day of the month of Adar, and on the fourteenth they rested and made it a day of feasting and joy.
>
> The Jews in Susa, however, had assembled on the thirteenth and fourteenth, and then on the fifteenth they rested and made it a day of feasting and joy.
>
> That is why rural Jews—those living in villages—observe the fourteenth of the month of Adar as a day of joy and feasting, a day for giving presents to each other.
>
> Mordecai recorded these events, and he sent letters to all the Jews throughout the provinces of King Xerxes, near and far, to have them celebrate annually the fourteenth and fifteenth days of the month of Adar as the time when the Jews got relief from their enemies, and as the month when their sorrow was turned into joy and their mourning into a day of celebration. He wrote them to observe the days as days of feasting and joy and giving presents of food to one another and gifts to the poor (Esther 9:17–22).

Notice the special character of this celebration: Again and again, we read that this was to be a day of joy and feasting. It was also to be a day of rest, so the people could reflect—remembering how they were delivered from the oppression of their enemies. It was to be celebrated by exchanging presents and giving gifts to the poor. All of these aspects of the Feast of Purim are symbols of the fruit of victory.

Looking at this story once more as a parable for our lives, what parallels do we find in this description of the Feast of Purim? Throughout the book, we have seen one parallel after another between the conflict in the story and the central conflict of the Christian life—the struggle to gain victory over the manifestations of the flesh. And just as the Feast of Purim celebrates and symbolizes the fruit of victory over the enemies of the Jews, we see in the Christian life the fruit of victory over the flesh and its manifestations. What is the fruit of victory in the Christian life called?

As we discussed earlier, it is the fruit of the Spirit.

The New Testament teaches that as we come to experience the way of the Spirit and the freedom of the Spirit in an ever-increasing way, the Spirit produces within us certain beautiful and godly traits called the fruit of the Spirit—love, joy, peace, patience, kindness, goodness, faithfulness, gentleness and self-control (see Galatians 5:22–23). These are the virtues of a life that is yielded to the control of the Holy Spirit. This fruit can come about only as we experience victory over the flesh through total dependence on Him. That is the first thing God wants us to remember.

What was life like for the Jewish people under Haman? He symbolized the rule of the flesh, the self-life, the unbridled ego, the uncrucified self within the believer. Life under Haman was unrelentingly miserable. There was no joy, no feasting, no gladness while Haman was in power—none whatsoever. While Haman ruled, the king was deceived and the kingdom was in confusion and despair.

Remember that at the end of Esther 3, when Haman convinced the king to issue the first decree, the entire city of Susa was bewildered by the king's actions. That is what happens when a Christian is ruled by the flesh—bewilderment and confusion. People expect a king to behave rationally—and people expect Christians to behave like Christians. When kings issue outrageous edicts and when Christians engage in outrageous behavior, the people around them are bewildered and confused.

Many Christians struggle to do their best for God, yet they have never learned how to rest in Him and depend upon the indwelling life of the Lord. Until we learn how to live by the Spirit, Haman remains in control. Our lives are confused and produce confusion in the people around us. We feel defeated and dejected and depressed, and we wonder why we experience no victory in our lives.

I'm not saying that a Christian who lives by the Spirit feels continuously, deliriously happy and never experiences any problems. Indeed, the deeper we go into the life of the Spirit, the greater our challenges and problems usually become. When we step up to the front lines of the spiritual battlefield, it is only natural that we would experience greater conflict, opposition, and suffering.

But in the midst of our difficult circumstances, God has promised us a supply of peace, joy, and victory. And what is victory? It is not freedom from sorrow, pressure, obstacles, or suffering. Rather, victory is that experience of an inner quietness, a sense of joy and gladness, of peace and rest, no matter how bleak our circumstances may seem. Our joy does not depend on our circumstances. It depends on our relationship with Jesus Christ. Our comfort does not come from money in the bank or material possessions. It comes from the Comforter himself, the Holy Spirit.

Jesus told us, "In this world you will have trouble. But take heart! I have overcome the world" (John 16:33). Obstacles and opposition are inevitable in this life, but our Lord Jesus is never taken by surprise. He has overcome every obstacle and opponent in our path, and He has given us the victory.

SECOND KEY TRUTH:
REMEMBER THE STEPS TO VICTORY

The next key truth God wants us to remember is how victory is achieved. In other words, God wants us to remember *the steps to victory*. We read:

> So the Jews agreed to continue the celebration they had begun, doing what Mordecai had written to them. For Haman son of Hammedatha, the Agagite, the enemy of all the Jews, had plotted against the Jews to destroy them and had cast the *pur* (that is, the lot) for their ruin and destruction. But when the plot came to the king's attention, he issued written orders that the evil scheme Haman had devised against the Jews should come back onto his own head, and that he and his sons should be hanged on the gallows (Esther 9:23–25).

134

It's important to give attention to how victory is achieved. This is true whether you are a Jew living five hundred years before Christ or a Christian living today. Most Christians know the feeling of falling into overwhelming circumstances and crying out to God for help. Inevitably, God responds to our desperate plea, and we experience deliverance and victory. But we tend to regard this intervention as "emergency assistance," available only when our back is against the wall.

In reality, we should view these kinds of emergencies as the normal condition of the Christian life. We were meant to always be in trouble—facing opposition and trials on a regular basis. Only through experiencing crisis after crisis do we experience the power of Christ resting on us. As an apostle Paul wrote, "We always carry around in our body the death of Jesus, so that the life of Jesus may also be revealed in our body" (2 Corinthians 4:10).

What is the situation for the Christian? A Christian is a person who is completely fearless and constantly in trouble. Opposition and obstacles are constant companions as the Christian goes through life. But as Jesus told us, we must take heart! Whenever we face conflict, God will provide the way to victory.

What are the steps to victory we see outlined in Esther 9? This passage forms a succinct summary of the book of Esther that outlines for us the steps to victory:

Step One: Know Your Enemy. The passage gives us Haman's name in full: "Haman son of Hammedatha, the Agagite, the enemy of all the Jews." His treachery has been fully exposed. He is a picture of the enemy within, the all-consuming self, the fleshly ambition for prominence and preeminence. The message of this first step is that we must recognize our enemy. That's not as easy as it sounds.

Our enemy doesn't always look like an enemy. He does not come wearing a red devil costume with horns and a sinuous tail. Our enemy comes to us in an alluring disguise, with a sweet voice, an attractive appearance, and a pleasing manner. And that is why our enemy is all the more deadly. It's difficult to recognize him as an enemy, because his voice sounds so sweet.

Jesus once asked His disciples, "Who do people say the Son of Man is?" In reply, they recounted some of the rumors that had been spread about Him. Then Jesus asked, "Who do *you* say I am?" Peter, moved by the Holy Spirit, replied, "You are the Christ [that is, the Messiah], the Son of the living God." Jesus said, in effect, "you're right, and you didn't learn this by yourself; my Father in heaven revealed it to you" (see Matthew 16:13–20).

Then Jesus began to teach the disciples about the road ahead. He told them He had to go to Jerusalem and be tried by the chief priests and scribes, then be slain upon the cross. On the third day, he would rise again. Peter couldn't stand to hear these things, so he took Jesus aside and said, "Never, Lord! This shall never happen to you!"

In reply, Jesus delivered a stinging rebuke—not to Peter, but to Satan, who had prompted those words by appealing to the fleshly side of Peter. "Get behind me, Satan!" Jesus said. "You are a stumbling block to me; you do not have in mind the things of God, but the things of men."

Satan, the enemy of our souls, was able to entice Peter into fleshly thinking immediately after Peter had made his wonderful profession of faith. Our two great enemies—Satan and the flesh—are subtle and deceptive, and we need to be taught by the Word to recognize their traps and strategies. That is the first step to victory.

Step Two: Live by the New Law. The second step to victory is the realization that a new decree has been issued, and we are no longer bound by the old decree. We read of the new decree in verse 25:

> But when the plot came to the king's attention, he issued written orders that the evil scheme Haman had devised against the Jews should come back onto his own head (Esther 9:25).

The new decree meant that the Jews were set free from the law of the old decree. This is a picture of our new life in Christ. Now that He dwells within us, we are set free from the law of sin and death. It is no longer up to us to work our way to God, constantly trying to be good, constantly trying to keep a set of rules and regulations, but never measuring up. The law has been replaced by grace. Our insufficient efforts have been replaced by His all-sufficient power.

Under the old law, we tried to show the world how much we can do for God. Under grace, with Christ living within us, we allow God to show the world all that He can do through us. We no longer have to struggle to be good. Instead, we live in dependence on the One who is good, who dwells within us, and whose life is made manifest through our lives. Our awareness of this life-giving, second decree is the second step to victory.

Step Three: Put Your Enemy to Death. The third step to victory is the hanging of Haman and his sons on the gallows. Look again at verse 25:

> But when the plot came to the king's attention, he issued written orders that the evil scheme Haman had devised against the Jews should come back onto his own head, and that he and his sons should be hanged on the gallows (Esther 9:25).

Until we are willing to put the old life to death, we never can lay hold of that indwelling life. Haman and Mordecai, the flesh and the Spirit, cannot coexist. The flesh has to go. If you hold back a portion of your ego as a private little area that you exclude from God, you cannot lay hold of the victory. True victory comes only when we agree to slay the self within us so that the life of Jesus may be manifested and expressed in our lives. The self-giving life of Christ must replace the self-serving life of the flesh.

That is the third and ultimate step to victory.

THIRD KEY TRUTH:
REMEMBER THE DURATION OF VICTORY

The third truth God wants us to remember is the duration of victory:

> (Therefore these days were called Purim, from the word *pur.*) Because of everything written in this letter and because of what they had seen and what had happened to them, the Jews took it upon themselves to establish the custom that they and their descendants and all who join them should without fail observe these two days every year, in the way prescribed and at the time appointed. These days should be remembered and observed in every generation by every family, and in every province and in every city. And these days

of Purim should never cease to be celebrated by the Jews, nor should the memory of them die out among their descendants.

So Queen Esther, daughter of Abihail, along with Mordecai the Jew, wrote with full authority to confirm this second letter concerning Purim. And Mordecai sent letters to all the Jews in the 127 provinces of the kingdom of Xerxes—words of goodwill and assurance—to establish these days of Purim at their designated times, as Mordecai the Jew and Queen Esther had decreed for them, and as they had established for themselves and their descendants in regard to their times of fasting and lamentation. Esther's decree confirmed these regulations about Purim, and it was written down in the records (Esther 9:26–32).

This passage tells us that victory must be celebrated regularly and remembered continually. The memory of victory must never die out. Only by continually recalling the victory can we remain free. If we ever forget how the victory was attained, the victory will be lost.

Just as the Jews remember the victory over their enemies through the annual Feast of Purim, we must continually remember our victory over the flesh through the cross of Jesus Christ. As soon as we forget how our victory over the flesh was attained, we are doomed to slip back into the domain of the self.

Victory is not a once-and-for-all event. Victory through the cross is a process that must continue throughout our lives. The initial experience of deliverance from the flesh is not the end but the beginning of a process that must go on and on as long as we live.

In the Jewish community, there is a tradition that says the Feast of Purim is the only feast that will continue to be observed after Messiah comes. Jews say that the feasts of Tabernacles and Passover and all the others will cease when Messiah comes, but the Feast of Purim will go on even in the days of the kingdom.

This tradition can remind us that walking in the Spirit is to be our continual way of life, both for time and eternity. We must teach this truth to our descendants as well, so that our children will know what it means to walk in victory over the deeds of the flesh: resentment, jealousy, impatience, envy, lust, self-love, self-pity, pride, and all the rest. This spiritual victory that the Lord has won in your life and mine will be lost in the next generation if we do not hand down the principles of victory to our children.

Over the years, I've seen many children grow up in Christian homes, only to enter young adulthood feeling bewildered and defeated because they have never learned how to walk in the Spirit. They have been raised in Sunday school, they have given their lives to Christ, but they have never learned how to experience victory over the flesh. Let us always remember to teach our children how to walk and grow in the Spirit, so that they might experience a lifetime of victory.

There is a fascinating Old Testament story about a man named Enoch, who had learned the secret of walking with God (see Genesis 5:21–24). In those days, when the world was young, people routinely lived for several centuries, and Enoch lived for 365 years—but at the end of that time, he did not die. Genesis 5:24 tells us, "Enoch walked with God; then he was no more, because God took him away." In other words, Enoch did not have to pass through death. He simply walked with God and walked with God until one day he walked straight into glory.

That is the picture of what God would have for all of us as believers in Christ. He wants us to experience victory—not just a moment of victory but a lifetime of victory. And the way we experience victory throughout our lives is by walking with God, step by step by step. We hold on to victory by remembering that victory is a process, not an event. Only by remembering the duration of victory can we live in victory throughout our lives.

FOURTH KEY TRUTH:
REMEMBER THE SECRET OF VICTORY

The book of Esther closes with the fourth great truth we should remember—the secret of victory:

> King Xerxes imposed tribute throughout the empire, to its distant shores. And all his acts of power and might, together with a full

account of the greatness of Mordecai to which the king had raised him, are they not written in the book of the annals of the kings of Media and Persia? Mordecai the Jew was second in rank to King Xerxes, preeminent among the Jews, and held in high esteem by his many fellow Jews, because he worked for the good of his people and spoke up for the welfare of all the Jews (Esther 10:1–3).

The final chapter, which is only three verses long, sums up the message of the entire book. The book of Esther began with King Xerxes as the prominent figure. In the opening scene in chapter 1, we saw the vast power and might of this ancient king.

But as we read on, we learned of a hidden cancer that was eating away at the heart of the kingdom. This cancer would, if left unchecked, destroy all the power and might of this king. Had the invisible hand of God not moved people and events, as recorded in this fascinating book, the king and his kingdom would have come to a terrible end. Apart from God's intervention, the tale of King Xerxes would have ended in tragedy, with death and loss and unimaginable sorrow.

Instead, the story of Queen Esther and King Xerxes concludes with the king depicted in all of his regal power and majesty, reigning in might over his far-flung empire. More important, the story concludes by showing us the power behind the throne of King Xerxes—Mordecai himself. Once he operated in the shadows, communicating with the queen through a secret messenger. Now he is known to all, second in rank to the king, and held in high esteem by the Jews.

As we have seen throughout this book, the king represents the human soul and Mordecai represents the Holy Spirit. We see that the activity of the Spirit in our lives mirrors the activity of Mordecai in the life of the king. In your life and mine, the will is supremely free to make decisions about everything that takes place in the kingdom. But there is a power behind the throne, and that power works through the will of the king. The Holy Spirit is the power in our lives, working to bring power and peace to the kingdom of our lives.

But the Holy Spirit never forces His will upon us. He does not manipulate us. He respects our freedom to choose our own way. When we permit

Him to fill our lives, when we rely upon His wisdom and guidance, then our kingdom is at peace, and His power becomes our power. That is a picture of the Spirit-filled life.

The open secret of every successful Christian is the Spirit-filled life. The Spirit-filled Christian is free—free to follow the Spirit's leading and free to do wrong if he chooses. But the Spirit-filled Christian has learned a profound lesson: The secret to victory in life lies in yielding one's will in continual dependence upon the Holy Spirit. When we place ourselves under the authority of God's Spirit, we receive His power, and we experience His peace and joy and all that we truly long for.

Through the power of the Holy Spirit, you and I can fall into a cesspool and come out smelling like a rose. Every circumstance works for good in our lives. No matter how painful and difficult our situation may be, God promises that He "causes all things to work together for good to those who love God, to those who are called according to His purpose" (Romans 8:28 NASB). For the Christian who is truly yielded to God, disappointments only make him better, not bitter. Heartaches become stepping stones to joy. Trials produce the choicest of virtues. Weakness becomes an opportunity to manifest God's strength. Ugly circumstances produce inner beauty.

That is the secret of the Spirit-filled life: Inadequate human beings, indwelt by the Spirit of God, meet every challenge fully supplied with God's adequate resources. The "secret" is no more complicated than that. It is simple, yet profound.

Through the cross of Christ, God has devised an ingenious solution to the problem of sin. He found a way to crucify the flesh within us without destroying us. The apostle Paul described God's solution in these uplifting words:

> I am crucified with Christ: nevertheless I live; yet not I, but Christ liveth in me: and the life which I now live in the flesh I live by the faith of the Son of God, who loved me, and gave himself for me (Galatians 2:20 KJV).

Through dependence upon Christ, the Haman within has been crucified and put to death, and we are filled with the Spirit of Christ. We live on as new creations, celebrating our victory over sin and the flesh. And Haman, the old flesh, hangs crucified as a reminder: Don't ever go back to what you once were. Keep yielding and yielding and yielding yourself to the increasing control of the Lord.

That is the secret to a life of never-ending victory in Christ.

12

FOR SUCH A TIME AS THIS

Concluding Reflections

These are turbulent, even apocalyptic days. We face constant threats from global terrorism, the nuclear menace, economic chaos, population pressure, environmental catastrophe, the breakdown of values and culture, and much more. Are these the Last Days?

We don't know. The timetable of history belongs to the Father alone. But we do know that we need to rely upon Him in these days as never before.

You might think that an ancient document like the book of Esther would be irrelevant in our Internet-speed age. Yet, as we have examined the story of Esther and Mordecai, we have seen that this story is more pertinent to our own time than at any other time in history. This is not merely a book about how God's people should respond to times of crisis. It is truly a book that can show us how to become the kind of men and women God uses for such a time as this.

Like the exiled Jews in Persia, we often feel helpless and powerless, caught in the grip of events beyond our control. We feel we have no power to influence events as our world seems to collapse around our ears.

The message of the book of Esther is that God has a part for each of us to play. It doesn't matter if the part God has assigned us is small or great. Every role is important in the grand drama now unfolding on the stage of world events. God has called each of us to do our part to advance His kingdom in these crucial times.

DEPENDING ON THE HOLY SPIRIT

We have examined the book of Esther chapter-by-chapter, scene-by-scene. Now let's take a final overview of it, paying attention to several specific themes of the book and how they apply to our lives in these uncertain times. Here is an outline of the story of Esther:

Part I: The Peril of Esther, Mordecai, and the Jews (Esther 1–4)

The king selects Esther as his queen	1:1–2:20
Haman's plot against Mordecai and the Jews	2:21–4:17

Part II: The Triumph of Esther, Mordecai, and the Jews (Esther 5–10)

Esther and Mordecai lay a trap for Haman	5
The king honors Mordecai	6
The execution of Haman	7
Mordecai receives the estate of Haman	8:1–3
Israel triumphs over her enemies	8:4–9:32
The eminence of Mordecai is recounted	10

Let's briefly review the story of Esther.

The story opens in the royal palace in Susa. In chapter 1, we meet King Xerxes, and we encounter the first of many parallels between the story of Esther and our own lives. We discover that we were created to be like a king. You and I each have a kingdom over which to rule—the kingdom of the soul, made up of the mind (our ability to think and reason), the emotions (our ability to feel), and the will (our ability to make choices and take action). As a king, you have an empire that includes everything within your sphere of influence.

When we meet King Xerxes, we see that he has nothing to do except host a six-month-long party to display the glory and splendor of his kingdom. This prideful king tries to humiliate his beautiful Queen Vashti by ordering her to display her beauty before his drunken guests. When the queen refuses his command, the king divorces Vashti, banishing her from the palace forever.

In chapter 2, the book of Esther introduces us to the title character, Esther herself. The theme of this portion of the story is, "Depending on the Holy Spirit."

After King Xerxes banishes Queen Vashti from the palace, he realizes he can't take back his decree. Yet, at the same time, he can't stand living alone. So he begins a search for a new queen. In the process, a young Jewish beauty is brought before him. Though her Hebrew name is Hadassah, she goes by the Persian name Esther.

Born in exile, Esther has never known her ancestral homeland in Palestine. After the death of her parents, she was raised by her cousin Mordecai. Having grown up in Persia, she has learned to talk and act like a Persian, so that no one even suspects that her heart belongs to the God of Abraham, Isaac, and Jacob.

These two central characters, Esther and Mordecai, form a profound and instructive symbolic image. Esther signifies the renewed spirit that is given to a person when he or she becomes a Christian. She represents a human spirit that has undergone regeneration, the new birth—the spirit that has been made alive in Christ.

Esther's cousin, Mordecai, is a picture of the Holy Spirit. His behind-the-scenes influence on Esther represents the influence and control of the Holy Spirit on the soul and spirit of a believer.

When King Xerxes meets Esther, he instantly falls in love with her and chooses her as his queen. So Esther is elevated from the status of an exile to that of the most honored and privileged woman in Persia. On Mordecai's advice, Esther withholds the truth of her Jewish parentage from the king.

The marriage between King Xerxes and Queen Esther is a symbolic picture of conversion. In essence, the king receives a new spirit (the queen), even though he has no awareness of Mordecai (who represents the Holy Spirit). The king symbolizes those Christians who have little or no understanding of what has happened to them at the moment they received Christ.

Mordecai is active and involved in the background of the story, but King Xerxes forgets his influence. A record of Mordecai's role in averting the assassination is recorded in the annals of the kingdom, however, and Mordecai's deed will not remain forgotten forever.

As we see these events taking shape, it is clear that even though God is not named in the text His influence suffuses every page and every paragraph of the story. Likewise, God is active in the events of our lives, even when we cannot see His hand nor hear His voice. So we need to learn to trust Him, even when we cannot detect His presence. And we need to learn to depend on the Spirit for wisdom, strength, and comfort—especially in troubled times when it is hard to sense God's presence.

EXPECT OPPOSITION, PERSECUTION, AND HATRED

Esther 3 introduces Haman, the villain of the story—a self-seeking, power-hungry official with Hitler-like tendencies. The theme of this section can be summed up with the Lord's words to His disciples: "In this world you will have trouble" (John 16:33). If you are a follower of Christ, you should expect opposition, persecution, and hatred from people like Haman.

The text tells us that Haman was descended from the Amalekites, a race of people who had continually made war against God and His people. Haman represents the corrupt flesh within us, the sinful nature that is constantly at war with God. Haman is subtle and crafty, and he continually plots to destroy Mordecai and the Jewish people.

A cunning strategist, Haman worms his way into the confidence of the king and rises to a place of prominence—an executive position equivalent to a modern-day prime minister. All the other noblemen of the palace bow the knee to Haman, feeding his ego by paying him honor. But Mordecai refuses to bow the knee before this tinhorn dictator. So Haman becomes enraged and swears revenge—not only against Mordecai, but against all of his people. Haman proceeds to plot murder—and genocide.

Haman, a master of political intrigue, controls the king the same way a puppeteer controls the puppet. Haman convinces the king to issue an edict to slaughter all the Jews. The king complies, completely unaware that his own wife, Queen Esther, is herself a Jew. That genocidal edict is the thematic turning point of the book. From this point on, the story focuses on how God removes one from power (the one who is in the wrong) and puts another person (the person who is in the right)—Mordecai—into power. In the process, God uses Mordecai and Esther to bring hope to a seemingly hopeless situation.

Why is Haman so consumed by hatred of the Jews? It goes much deeper than Haman's rage against Mordecai. In Esther 3:8, Haman tells the king that the customs of the Jewish people "are different from those of all other people." In other words, the Jews obey a different life principle than the customs of the Persians. Whereas the Persians are pagan idolaters, the Jews worship the one true God—and Haman, as an Agagite and an Amalekite, is an enemy of God and His people. He hates the Jews because they are God's uniquely chosen people and because they live their lives according to God's own moral and spiritual principles.

What does Haman's ancient hatred have to do with us today? Actually, quite a lot. People have not changed in 2,500 years. They still hate those who operate by a different life principle, who obey a different rule of living, and who bow the knee to God and not to petty tyrants.

If you choose to follow Jesus Christ and live in dependence on the Holy Spirit, you will soon find yourself hated and even persecuted. If you choose to live a moral and upright life, and let the light of your faith shine before men and women in the world around you, you will become a target. You will be subject to attack by those who wallow in the moral filth of this dying world. If you truly live like a follower of Jesus Christ, you're going to sparkle like a diamond on a coal pile. By your conspicuous godliness, you invite persecution from those whose deeds are evil.

How can you stand up to the opposition and persecution that comes to you as a follower of Christ? You need the courage of Esther and the wisdom of Mordecai. You can stand against those challenges by the same life principle that Esther and Mordecai relied upon. All the courage you need, all the wisdom you lack is available to you through dependence on the Spirit of God.

COURAGE FOR THE BATTLE

In chapter 4, we see God's invisible hand setting events in motion—and we see Mordecai and Esther cooperating with God's plan and offering themselves to be used for His purpose. With a messenger named Hathach as a go-between, Mordecai explains Haman's plot against the Jews to Queen Esther. When Esther hears the details of the plot, she is devastated—but not immobilized. Mordecai urges her to approach the king on behalf of the Jews—and Esther agrees to the daring plan.

Mordecai has just asked Esther to take the most dangerous risk imaginable. She must go boldly into the presence of the moody and unpredictable king without being summoned—an act that incurs the death sentence if the king is displeased. But Esther agrees to take the risk. "If I perish, I perish," she says resignedly. Here we see the courage of the queen on full display. She puts her life on the line for the sake of her people—and she does so with a calm and resolute courage.

We have to ask ourselves: Where does that kind of courage come from? The times in which we live certainly call for that same kind of courage and resolute faith. Have you asked God for the courage to speak the truth of the gospel to your friends and neighbors? Have you asked Him for courage to oppose evil and take a stand for righteousness? Have you asked him for courage to be a witness for Christ in your workplace or your school?

As the world grows darker, the people around you need to see the light of Jesus Christ within you. Wherever God has placed you, ask Him to use your life to shed His light on the people around you. As Jesus said, "You are the light of the world. . . . Let your light shine before men, that they may see your good deeds and praise your Father in heaven" (Matthew 5:14, 16). Let the love of God and the light of God shine through your words and deeds.

PREPARE FOR SPIRITUAL WARFARE

When you ask God for the courage to make a stand for Him, be sure you are prepared for the challenge. Invest time in prayer and preparation, as Esther did when she fasted for three days and nights before going to see the king. Also, ask your Christian friends to lift you up in prayer to the Father. When Esther prepared herself to go before the king, she called upon Mordecai and all the Jews to fast and pray on her behalf.

On the third day, Esther goes before the king. She is fearful, but fear does not stop her. She is uncertain, but uncertainty does not hold her back. She steps forth boldly—and her boldness is rewarded. The king is delighted by her presence, he extends his scepter, and the queen captures his heart.

The king offers to grant Esther anything she wants, up to half the kingdom. Esther, in obedience to Mordecai's orders, bides her time. She leaves the king hanging. Even more important, she gives Haman the opportunity to hang himself by his own cruel folly.

We see a vitally important principle in this section of the story of Esther: Never go into battle without being fully prepared.

Esther was engaged in warfare—spiritual warfare. Her husband, the king, had been taken prisoner by the satanic schemes of Haman. She was battling Haman for the mind and heart of her deceived husband. She had to say the exactly the right words and do all the right things or the war would be lost—and her people would be slaughtered.

You and I are also engaged in spiritual warfare. We are battling Satan for the minds and hearts of our families, our children, our friends and neighbors. Those around you who don't know the Lord Jesus Christ are held captive by this fallen world and the invisible rulers who control it. Our enemy is not a human being or a human political system or a human ideology. Our enemy is a cruel and powerful kingdom of spiritual forces, led by Satan.

Before we go up against such a powerful enemy, we need to prepare ourselves mentally, morally, and spiritually—just as Esther did. We need to spend time in prayer and Scripture study, seeking the wisdom, strength, and will of God. And we need to ask others to pray for us, counsel us, and encourage us for the struggle. Paul put it this way:

> Finally, be strong in the Lord and in his mighty power. Put on the full armor of God so that you can take your stand against the devil's schemes. For our struggle is not against flesh and blood, but against the rulers, against the authorities, against the powers of this dark world and against the spiritual forces of evil in the heavenly realms. Therefore put on the full armor of God, so that when the day

of evil comes, you may be able to stand your ground, and after you have done everything, to stand (Ephesians 6:10–13).

Follow the example of Queen Esther. Remember that this life is a battlefield, and you must never go into battle unprepared.

DESTROY THE FLESH

Meanwhile the battle between Haman and Mordecai continues. Mordecai refuses to bow before the egotistical Haman. Just as the Holy Spirit is not impressed with human arrogance, Mordecai is neither impressed nor intimidated by the arrogance of Haman. As a result, Haman grows ever more enraged at Mordecai's refusal to pay him homage. Haman's friends counsel him to destroy Mordecai—to build a gallows, a high impaling post, and to crucify Mordecai upon it.

Isn't that just like the flesh? "If people get in your way," the flesh says to us, "don't go around them—go *through* them. Destroy them. Obliterate them. Make them sorry they were ever born." The flesh is cruel and relentlessly self-centered.

At this point, Mordecai's cause seems lost—at least, from a human perspective. There is no prospect of help coming from any direction. Mordecai has no power, except the limited influence he can wield through Esther. The king's edict of death for the Jewish people hangs over the nation and cannot be reversed. There seems to be no hope.

But God is taking a hand. He is moving events in ways that neither Mordecai nor Esther can foresee. Though God is not mentioned by name, he directly intervenes by troubling the sleep of King Xerxes. The king, in his insomnia, orders his attendants to read from the annals of the kingdom.

And there he hears the story of an attempt against his life—and he recalls that the conspiracy was thwarted by Mordecai and reported by Queen Esther. The king realizes that Mordecai has never been properly honored for his service to the king.

Meanwhile, God sovereignly ordains that Haman should choose that exact time to enter the king's court. Haman intends to persuade the king to order Mordecai's execution. Through a brilliant twist of irony that only God himself could have engineered, Haman's plan is turned on its head—and Haman, the man who craves honor *from* Mordecai, is forced to give honor *to* Mordecai—his hated enemy, his intended victim!

Later, King Xerxes, Esther, and Haman come together over dinner. During the meal, the king asks Queen Esther to name her request. She replies, "If it pleases your majesty, grant me my life—this is my petition. And spare my people—this is my request. For I and my people have been sold for destruction and slaughter and annihilation" (Esther 7:3–4). Then Queen Esther reveals that the man behind the plot to destroy the Jews is Haman himself.

When the king realizes that he has been manipulated and deceived by Haman, he orders Haman's execution. So Haman is nailed to the very gallows he had prepared for Mordecai. The king hands Haman's entire estate over to Esther, who entrusts it to Mordecai. The king then elevates and exalts Mordecai, making him second in influence and power only to the king himself.

The exaltation of Mordecai symbolizes the fullness of the Spirit, the moment when we give God's Spirit His rightful place in our lives. This is a picture of the fullness of the Spirit.

Throughout the Book of Esther, Mordecai has symbolized the Holy Spirit in the life of a believer. We see the activity of the Spirit in various stages at different points in the story:

Passage	Event	Symbolism
Esther 2	*Advised by Mordecai, Esther becomes queen*	The Spirit received
Esther 3	*Angered by Mordecai, Haman plots to kill the Jews*	The Spirit resisted
Esther 4:1–3	*Mordecai mourns in sackcloth and ashes*	The Spirit grieved
Esther 4:4	*Esther sends clothes to quench Mordecai's grief*	The Spirit quenched

Passage	Event	Symbolism
Esther 4:5–17	*Esther listens to Mordecai and obeys*	Led by the Spirit
Esther 6	*The king recalls that Mordecai saved his life*	The Spirit honored
Esther 8	*The king exalts Mordecai as prime minister*	Fullness of the Spirit

When Mordecai comes to power, everything changes. Instantly, the king issues a second decree, giving the Jews the right to defend themselves and destroy their enemies. By means of the ascendancy of Mordecai, the Jews are freed from the old decree of death. Paul, in Romans, sums up the theme of Esther:

> For what the law was powerless to do in that it was weakened by the sinful nature, God did by sending his own Son in the likeness of sinful man to be a sin offering. And so he condemned sin in sinful man, in order that the righteous requirements of the law might be fully met in us, who do not live according to the sinful nature [i.e., the Haman-minded flesh] but according to the Spirit [being Mordecai-minded] (Romans 8:3–4).

The choice that confronts us every day of our lives is a stark decision: Shall I follow the flesh, or shall I follow the Spirit? Shall I pattern my life after Haman, or shall I pattern my life after the Spirit-led guidance of Mordecai?

We live in challenging, turbulent, perilous times. But don't let the headlines frighten you. Don't let wars and rumors of wars shake your confidence in God. Don't let the actions of terrorists or despots or corrupt politicians trouble your sleep. Don't let the ups and downs of the stock market or the consumer price index fill you with dread or panic.

God is in control today, just as He was in control of events in Persia during Queen Esther's time. God's name wasn't mentioned even once in the story, yet His invisible hand was moving throughout the kingdom of

Persia, orchestrating events and working through people. He caused even the actions of evil men to serve His purpose and accomplish His plan.

And now our Lord calls us to report for duty. He has a plan for our lives. He has a mission for us to perform in our world today. If we belong to Him, then His Spirit is within us, counseling us, comforting us, preparing us, supplying us with all the wisdom and strength we need to fulfill His strategy for our lives.

God has positioned you where you are, in this special place, at this unique moment in time, so you can fulfill your part in His eternal plan. He has called and commissioned you. The Spirit of God now asks you the same question Mordecai asked of Esther: Who knows but that you have been placed in this strategic position for such a time as this?

What will your answer be?

NOTES

Chapter 1. I Am Only One

1. Martin Luther, quoted in *The Cyclopædia of Biblical Literature*, ed. by John Kitto (New York: Ivison & Phinney, 1854), p. 663.

Chapter 2. A Pair of Queens

1. Charles Don Keyes, *Brain Mystery, Light and Dark* (New York: Routledge, 1999), p. 10.

2. Nancy K. Frankenberry, *The Faith of Scientists* (Princeton, New Jersey: Princeton University Press, 2008), p. 372.

Chapter 3. Queen Esther and Mordecai

1. Clifton Fadiman, editor, *The Little, Brown Book of Anecdotes* (New York: Little, Brown, 1985), p. 191.

Chapter 9. The Law of the Spirit

1. Mark Bowden, "Tales of the Tyrant," *Atlantic Monthly*, May 2002, retrieved at http://www.theatlantic.com/doc/200205/bowden.

NOTE TO THE READER

The publisher invites you to share your response to the message of this book by writing Discovery House Publishers, P.O. Box 3566, Grand Rapids, MI 49501, U.S.A. For information about other Discovery House books, music, videos, or DVDs, contact us at the same address or call 1-800-653-8333. Find us on the Internet at http://www.dhp.org/ or send an e-mail to books@dhp.org.